Advance Praise for Wayward Tracks

In this wonderful crazy quilt of short essays and poems, Mark Collins takes us on a bumpy ride along his neural highways, with plenty of stops along the way to plunge deeply and perceptively into the everyday holiness of our lives.

Paul Wilkes, author, *Your Second Last Chapter*

Mark Collins is a sneaky good essayist, I think, funny and sad and witty and piercing all at once.

Brian Doyle, author, *So Very Much the Best of Us,*
and editor, *Portland Magazine,* University of Portland

This is a guy book, by a guy, for guys. Gals might like it, too, but only if they really want to know how we guys feel about the things we actually think about.

Greg Pierce, author, *The Spirituality of Work*

WAYWARD TRACKS

Mark Collins

Revelations about fatherhood, faith, fighting with your spouse, surviving Girl Scout camp, striking bottom, hitting fifty, playing hockey, trick knees, fugitive joy, looking for your car keys, fixing what's broken, first sonograms, last goodbyes, and remembering what matters most.

in extenso

WAYWARD TRACKS
by Mark Collins

Edited by Michael Coyne
Design and typesetting by Patricia A. Lynch
Front cover photo by Lisa Solonynko Photography
Back cover photo by Kathryn Hyslop Photography

Published by In Extenso Press

Distributed exclusively by ACTA Publications, 4848 N. Clark Street, Chicago, IL 60640, (800) 397-2282, www.actapublications.com

Poems previously appeared in the chapbook *Thank You for Your Submission*. (Pudding House Chapbook Series, © Mark Collins 2007)

All devotions by Mark Collins that originally appeared in *Daily Guideposts* are reprinted with permission from Guideposts Books. Copyright © 2000, 2005, 2006, 2008, 2010, 2011 by Guideposts. All rights reserved.

The author would like to thank the *Pittsburgh Post-Gazette*, the *Wisconsin Review*, *The Pitt News* and *Pitt Magazine*, where some of these poems and essays first appeared.

Library of Congress Catalog Number: 2016937871
Paperback ISBN: 978-0-87946-986-3
Printed in the United States of America by Total Printing Systems
Year 25 24 23 22 21 20 19 18 17 16
Printing 15 14 13 12 11 10 9 8 7 6 5 4 3 2 First

♻ Text printed on 30% post-consumer recycled paper.

PLAYLIST

FOREWORD

By Paul Wilkes
Author, *Your Second to Last Chapter*

Laundry Lists of Stupid Stuff

Most of our lives are spent churning over old hates and loves and replaying videos that have some semblance to what really happened but are mostly highly edited versions of the truth. Usually that's where the Rorschach of our lives remain, running up and down the neural highways, howling at the moon, sobbing uncontrollably or laughing like a fool.

For some of us, the writers among us, those brain meanderings find their way to the tips of our fingers and onto a page. We ask ourselves: Is it only me? Am I the only one with a laundry list of stupid stuff scrolling through my mind as if my finger was stuck on the keyboard's down arrow?

We write about what we have experienced and what we think about what we have experienced. Yes, we want to entertain our readers, but I believe we mostly want to remind ourselves what we really saw, felt, and did. We want our memories to come clear, and the only way to do that is to write them down. And, looking at our written words, we often find that "Yes, that's exactly the way it was, the mythic truth, far clearer than it ever was before in my befuddled brain."

Mark Collins is a very good writer. In this wonderful crazy quilt of short essays and poems, he takes us on a bumpy ride along his neural highways, with plenty of stops along the way to plunge deeply and perceptively into the everyday holiness of our lives. (Sample of his tone: "I speak to you as a happily married man. I can't speak for my wife Sandee, because she's not speaking to me right now.")

We hear of Mark's father, whose mother pleaded successfully to FDR to keep her son out of World War II, only to see him enlist. We examine the contents of the glove compartment of his car about to be sold that tell exactly who this fellow is. We read his letters to his daughter and to the pope and stories about death, life, banality, spirituality, faith, doubt…. They're all here, but lifted up with an indomitable spirit and literary skill we cannot help but cheer on: Go, Mark, go! Don't give up; you're on the one yard line; punch it home!

Now let me get out of the way and give you a preview of just a few of my favorite passages from *Wayward Tracks* by this Pittsburgh Everyman, who always provides us with a new spiritual, albeit sometimes painful, insight into the human encounters we readily recognize from our own life:

"*Maybe I'll try loving my neighbor by helping to load her cart at the supermarket instead of secretly seething because she has way more than twelve items in the express lane.*"

"*It has always troubled me that out of the five members of my birth family, I was the sixth-best writer. Everyone, including the dog, told better stories. My sister Cindy could tell stories—or at least finish them. When she found out that a well-known philanderer had lost his legs to diabetes, Cindy said, 'Well, he won't be running around on his wife anymore.'*"

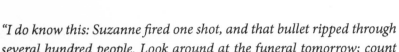

"I do know this: Suzanne fired one shot, and that bullet ripped through several hundred people. Look around at the funeral tomorrow; count the wounded. They'll be easy to spot. Suzanne loved her family, so I can only guess she wasn't herself when she picked up that gun."

"In the hierarchy of sin, the basest level is denying God's merciful bounty to our fellow astronauts on spaceship Earth. To squander the future for the present denies hope for God's children in coming generations. Trust me: There is a special circle in Hell (or at least a very long line in Purgatory) for souls with such hubris. Catholic or not, Christian or not, believer or not, we can't steal from the future and not pay the price. Nature always wins."

"And I've spent twice that time in church—an eternity, really—waiting and praying for miracles and answers. On days like today, sitting bumper-to-bumper on the Parkway East on my (late) way to work, prayer seems like an ill-timed joke and God reminds me of a careless absentee landlord who's put me up in a windowless, cold-water flat with no heat and no chance at subletting—except maybe to my sister in the ICU, who'd welcome the change."

"But that's not the end of it. All of these lonely, painful journeys share something else: shedding your old self. Not only shedding the usual suspects (possessions, prepossessions, presumptions), but shedding your old way of thinking.... Here is my prayer for you, the same prayer I whisper into the ether for myself: Pray to the God who's there. Pray to the God who you wish were there. Pray to the divine emptiness you feel."

INTRODUCTION

Words Fail Me, and Vice Versa

What happens when one's professional writing career is unforgivingly staked, in part, to the divine?

I worked as a writer for the better part of fifteen years before moving on to my current profession as a teacher and advisor. Writing was always more than just a job to me. Writing drove, enlightened, and finally devoured me. I gave it up mostly because writing and me weren't getting along. We had a passionate love affair, but a troubled marriage; finally we decided on a conscious uncoupling. Yet, like any old habit, it was never really gone. Recently I've made a new and disturbing discovery—it's not that I'm incompatible with language, it's that I don't trust it. My faith in words has faltered. For any serious writer "words fail me" isn't a cliché, it's a diagnosis.

Though I no longer write to put food on my family's table, and confess to being somewhat piety impaired, I continue to contribute to *Daily Guideposts*, a mainstream publication of inspirational devotionals. Some of what I have written for *Daily Guideposts*, newspapers, magazines and other publications is included here.

But any book claiming to be about divinity and honesty owes its readership full disclosure:

I believe in God. I think.

This acknowledgement alone is hilarious because my belief, tentative as it is, has not slowed down my repeated and active commission of sins. Although we all sin, some of us sin more spectacularly than others, and none more than those who write about it. To openly acknowledge one's belief *and* one's myriad transgressions is to secretly hope for public absolution. *He's self-flagellating in public! How refreshingly sincere!*—thus encouraging the sin of pride. How ironic.

Speaking of irony: memoirs such as these are, by nature, selfish and arrogant. The world is full of suffering in need of my hand and yours, yet here we both are, focusing on the first-world problems of a first-world sinner, a chronicle of irony and self-deception. Consider what follows to be a form of penance for this.

We used to think that humans were the only species that could use tools...until we saw other primates at work, and realized that was a stupid assumption. (That would have made a good working title for Darwin's *Origin of the Species: Human Pride—Another Stupid Assumption.*) Then we thought we were the only species to use language, and were proven wrong yet again. All sorts of species communicate, and those who do often seem to do it better than we humans. Have you ever watched a nature program about whales where one whale says to another, "Huh?" or "Wha'd you say?" *No.* They communicate over acres of ocean and never repeat themselves or mishear anything. Meanwhile I haven't understood one word Bob Dylan has sung in fifty years.

However, it is true—probably—that humans have some singular aspects in the ways we communicate: We're the only species that uses written language, we're the only species that understands irony, and we're the only species that deceives itself.

Granted, other species have a sense of humor, but it's pretty basic. Monkeys and chimps at the zoo fling things they shouldn't fling and laugh about it. (I'm laughing too but that's different. It's research.) But humans enjoy the richness of irony. Humans understand—occasionally, usually suddenly—that things aren't as they appear, and we're not who we think we are, and it's...well, not always amusing, but it's at least enlightening. *That's* irony. Irony is a blunt tool because irony is rude. Irony is truth-telling. Irony is unsettling.

To understand irony is to stare into the abyss, and see the abyss stare back and chuckle. With irony, you understand that life, even in its blackest form, is something of a joke; what seems to be Crucially Important is just a Passing Moment. The truth of your real rank in the world is restored. Your previous posture of consequence was just Another Stupid Assumption.

Other species also are good at deception—in fact, it's pretty much standard policy in nature to hide or camouflage oneself. They don't call it deception; they call it survival. No one rebukes a chameleon for changing colors. Humans, on the other hand, actually come up with lies of all sizes to deceive ourselves. *Ourselves.* Think about that. And forget the measly one-time lie—we create the kind of self-deceit that's a chronic, ongoing enterprise. We have built a narrative house of cards that we could easily break out of at any time, and yet we cannot imagine escape. *My spouse will never look at another person. My kids will always respect me. I will always do unto others…*do I need to go on? What I'm *really* saying is that my spouse will never be human, my kids will never be human, and I will never be human. Why would Jesus bother to become "fully human" if not to realize who and what we are? What would be the point? Surely some of the motivation would be to see our own brokenness—otherwise the Apostles' Creed is just Another Stupid Assumption, and Jesus never could have been "true God and true man" and never wrestled with the demons of self-deceit. On the contrary, Jesus *openly* wrestled with demons. He was just more successful at it than we are. (And while we're at it, it seems that Jesus was especially prickly about self-deceivers: "…one of you will betray me; you, you over there, will deny me three times." Not me, pal. No sir. You can count on me. Yep. Roger. You betcha.)

What did we humans do to deserve this unique good-and-bad combo-platter of deceit and irony? I can see the evolutionary advantage of deceit, both self- and otherwise. There are lots of instances in which the dishonest among us get the upper hand. But what evolutionary mechanism would select for irony? I can't figure it out, except that it apparently became important to us hominids to occasionally acknowledge that we aren't who we appear to be and that we are often, in fact, ridiculous. To admit this, I think, brings us to the outskirts of the divine, bordering on redemption: It announces something greater than the fatuous, self-important role humanity has assumed for itself. Maybe that's why we tend to celebrate the divine through art, literature, dance, theater, and poetry. It's difficult to achieve deep insight through our public or private selves. We have to make up personas to do the heavy lifting required of clear-eyed truth. It is through art that we edit our real selves. Our flesh-and-blood versions are lousy and evolving first drafts, with all the attendant sloppiness and misdirection and deceptive veneer.

Good writing *sounds* original, like hearing Louis Armstrong riff for the first time. But good writing is anything but original. Good writing cycles through countless iterations to parade as original; it rehearses and rehearses and rehearses to sound new. Many religions, especially Christianity, understand this. The "re-" prefix in redemption and resurrection implies a return to an earlier, purer, sinless state—but we all understand that's a ruse. We won't be returning to Eden ever, yet we live as if every Christmas is the first Christmas, every Easter is the first Easter, every new sin invites the possibility of new salvation: to revise ourselves, to seek redemption, again and again and again.

In reality, every act of revision in art is an act of contrition—thus the following prayer to me and to you, dear reader: *O My God, I am heartily sorry for this imperfect mess. I detest ridiculous, clichéd piety, sentimental and dishonest and cloying, which hath offended thee and me and everyone else. I am truly sorry and humbly repent, and firmly resolve to do better tomorrow—after at least six hours of sleep and a couple of shots of near-occasion, 80-proof, single-malt sin.*

Every act of revision is voluntary, like asking for forgiveness. Despite the advice from pop psychologists, most of us act as if it's *always* better to *not* ask for forgiveness and simply pretend everything is all right. Sure. We do the same with our words. Self-deception is so much easier than the hard work of truth-telling. We discern that our deathless prose is actually a little trite and dodgy. But they're okay for now, right? We firmly resolve to do better tomorrow, knowing tomorrow will require its own contrition.

And maybe that's why some of our favorite art portrays us as the hilarious, screwed-up, sinful characters that we are. That I am. I'm the person laid bare in the following pages, albeit revised and somewhat PhotoShopped, by my editors and by myself. But I think the whole idea of editing, revisiting, correcting, makes me all the more hopeful, makes the idea of redemption all the more possible, all the more holy, all the more amen.

TRACK 1

Mourning Has Broken

Sometimes life shatters.

At first there's the shock of the sudden, the wide-eyed *"what was that?"* followed by disbelief, then belief, then a numbness so deep that your heart beats but generates no measurable pulse. Time goes on, but you wouldn't know. Each morning you get up and get dressed—or not.

But at some point you have to address the pieces that are left, scattered about like an exploded jigsaw puzzle. And there you are on your knees, retrieving each piece—the big ones, the broken ones, the slivers. Slowly you rebuild the entire thing until your knees hurt and it still doesn't look anything like the picture on the box because of all that's missing. And all you can *think* about is what's missing, the sorrow of what isn't, the grief for what's gone.

And so, a choice: fill those voids using the tools you have around the house (memory, imagination, stubbornness, and maybe even prayer if you still can but no one would blame you if you can't), *or* focus forever on what might have been. I think that choice matters, maybe because there's just that one thing left that you control.

Eventually what you find in your hands isn't what's missing, but the unedited, un-cropped, un-filtered version of the photo on the box—the real version, the to-scale version, *your* version. Turns out this actual version will always have pieces missing, and missed...but the puzzle is now complete, holes and all. This holey puzzle is yours to keep.

Strangely, reality doesn't care how your new puzzle compares to the old picture. Reality doesn't notice what's missing, only what's there. In fact, most people won't notice what's missing, either, and you'll be thankful for that. Most people are kind, and those who aren't kind usually have more missing than you do.

There is some solace, I believe, in this journey. I have found such journeys begin not with a single step (that comes later), but begin at that initial moment—on your knees, trying to figure out what's lost, what's still here, trying to gather it all up, trying to gather the strength to start anew...

...and you think maybe hope has arrived, but it hasn't really because hope doesn't arrive on schedule or in a box. Hope comes the second you utter its name, the second you're willing to think about tomorrow, to plan again, to re-introduce yourself to your roommates on this planet, to live this new, unsought life as something both holey and holy.

Scribes once called these things faith and grace—the unseen, the undeserved—but these were compromise words, names to describe the unnamable, the indescribable. Somewhere deep in our marrow lies the steely will to move on when there's no earthly reason to do so. Our species has survived on such deep and fragile resilience, which resurrects itself each time we begin on our knees, looking finally past ourselves to what lies beyond what's missing to what we actually have, and what we can do for others with what we actually have.

And that's what a prayer is, I think.

TRACK 2 > PURGATORY ON WHEELS

TRACK 2A

Buddha in the Breakdown Lane

For centuries theologians have wondered how the world's great teachers—Buddha, Therese of Lisieux, the Desert Fathers, et.al.—were able to lead lives of such compassion and forgiveness.

I know how: None of them ever drove a car. Trust me—if the Buddha had my daily commute through rush hour in Pittsburgh he wouldn't be so jolly.

I admit my sins are many, and impatience ranks right up there. I look calm and collected behind the wheel, but I'm actually contemplating the logistics of a roof-mounted howitzer (sure it's costly, but I could then take care of the Camry that just cut me off for the fifth time).

Recently, however, I've tried another tack: praying. I already use the Lord's name in many colorful and creative ways, but this is different. I pray the rosary, which takes me from the Camp Horne entrance of I-279 all the way to town. There's something soothing, something comforting, something ineffable about this ancient litany of prayers, this connection with our storied past. I can't explain it—I just do it because it works.

Which might help explain that whole compassion and forgiveness thing, too.

TRACK 2B

None of Them Can Stop the Time

Last month I shooed my kids into the van and drove around the block. After a couple of circuits, I told them they were about to witness history: the odometer turned 200,000 miles.

They were less than impressed. "Does that mean we can buy a new car now?" my daughter Hope asked.

It's a fair question, because the van is in less than fair shape. The sliding door doesn't really close, which makes for a frosty ride. The "check engine" light is on permanently; sometimes it flashes three dots/three dashes/three dots. Where's that owner's manual? The rain gutter is loose—at high speeds it beats out a rhythm reminiscent of early Bob Marley.

And the whole idea of miles (even a nice round number) is suspect. In case you're curious—and even if you're not—the concept of miles is based on old English agrarian measurements (four rods per chain, eighty chains per mile). It's so bizarre that even the English have abandoned miles in favor of kilometers, so a celebration of 200,000 miles is about as meaningful as commemorating 1:23 p.m. because it only comes once a day.

Which got me thinking: chances are that the odometer is not accurate—see above—but it's still an achievement, right? That's like six trips around the globe. I might have reached the moon in another 40,000 miles. Since my van was born, we've had three presidents. Two of my three children were born, too, as were millions of other kids. People were married, divorced, lost jobs, found five dollars in the lint tray, got sick, got better, played hearts, had their hearts broken. In that same time period, I've kept the van together with an artful combination of body putty, mechanical ingenuity, and blue language. I've kept my life together too—no small feat—through pandemonium, therapy, and more blue language. Last year the deadline came and went, and no IRS audit—hallelujah! My sister can maneuver her wheelchair by simply turning her head, and not even God saw that coming.

It's funny how we celebrate arbitrary dates but rarely celebrate the fantastically wonderful mundane of today, of this afternoon, of now. Your youngest kid can read and write—do you have any idea what a gift that is? The roof will stay on your house through the next storm because of the good work of a carpenter you've never met. Tonight a four-year-old and a soldier in Iraq and a surgical nurse and a truck driver and your cousin Lenny will say a prayer, and it will be answered. And my van will start, I think, and I will be thrilled as I inch my way (not millimeter my way) through traffic toward home—a little cold, limping toward the next ordinary extraordinary milestone, listening hard to a Bob Marley song about redemption.

It Takes a Village with a Trouble Light

Our van is…um, *well-known* in the neighborhood. It's sixteen years old, with 200,000 miles on it and enough rust to qualify as two-toned. My kids call the van by its given name: That Thing, as in "are you still driving That Thing?"

About a month ago, That Thing went belly-up. I assumed the worst, and spent many evenings in tandem pursuits: either underneath the van with an orange trouble light and a red hot temper, or kvetching with family and friends. Finally, I repaired the bad radiator/leaky valve cover/dirty transmission filter/wayward ignition wire, and the van was back on the road.

My wife was impressed. "You fixed it yourself," Sandee said.

Yes. Yes, I did. No. No, I didn't. I did the work, but Sandee had pointed out the original (and subtle) leak. My brother recommended a compression test, and told me where to buy a kit. Mr. D suggested the cooling system as the culprit. Megan let me borrow her truck, even though she needed it herself. My kids took turns holding flashlights and handing me tools. My next-door neighbor loaned me the perfect snub-nosed wrench. Parents who ordinarily didn't carpool with our kids suddenly appeared, ready to help. And when I fixed the van, they all said congrats.

For what? It took a village to fix my ancient van. It takes a village to fix all sorts of ancient, intractable problems: broken cars, broken hearts, broken lives, broken politics. I can't reattach the #4 plug myself, but if you hold the trouble light, we can do it together. It seems impossible, but together—trust me—we can do it. Together.

TRACK 2D

The Last of How It Was

Found in the glove box in the ancient family van before it was auctioned off for charity:

1) Albuterol Bronchodilator

For bronchitis—a gift my children once gave me. How thoughtful.

2) One-Year Muffler Warranty, Plus the Bill for Installation and State Inspection

When I can't do this kind of work myself—mufflers, brake jobs—I pay someone else to do it, and complain about the price. At least I still change my own oil. (Note to self: The Nissan is way overdue.)

3) A Pen from the Seelbach Hotel

That's all it says—Seelbach Hotel. No address. They're not a local hotel, so God knows how many unwitting people's hands this pen has passed through to get to me. Now I'll wittingly pass it along to someone else.

4) A Coupon for Thirty-five Cents Off Cup-a-Soup

Don't like soup cups. Don't know why I have this. Think I'll throw it away.

5) A Map of the Pittsburgh Children's Museum

From our first visit—seems like centuries ago. Our eight-year-old daughter got lost on the third floor. "I thought you left me," she said when we found her. I remember saying the same thing to my parents once. How to explain the depth of feeling I have for this child? Does she know that her mother and I would gladly lay down our lives for her? Or does she only remember the consternation in our voices?

6) An Access Card to My Building at the University of Pittsburgh
I also have a key to the elevator. But what's there to steal? A pen from the Seelbach Hotel?

7) Three Crayola Crayons: Yellow (Broken), Orchid, and Violet
These used to keep Grace, our youngest, occupied in her car seat. When I was a kid, Crayola had a color called "flesh." I remember thinking, "This looks *nothing* like flesh." Imagine how a non-Caucasian child felt.

8) A Phone Number Written on a Scrap of Paper (No Name)
Probably a student of mine. I hope he/she got whatever guidance was required. I'm too embarrassed to call and say, "This is Mark Collins. And you are...?"

9) A Yarmulke from the Schugar Funeral Home
From the service for Claryne, my friend Ralph's mom. I didn't feel like out-of-place *goyim* until they chanted the *Kaddish* around the grave. Then I felt alone. *I lack the language to say goodbye,* I thought. Of course, my ignorance of Hebrew isn't the problem. I've been attending more and more funerals as my friends' parents pass away one by one. There is no language for these goodbyes.

Five weeks after that funeral, I wore my yarmulke again: We attended the bris of Ralph's new baby boy, Caleb—one huge life event tailgating another. It's hard not to think in clichés at times like these; I kept remembering Claryne's favorite song from *Fiddler on the Roof:* "Sunrise, Sunset."

Shalom, Clare. Next year in Jerusalem.

10) Two Mismatched Kids' Gloves

Note to self: Isn't there an oddly similar pair on Hope's dresser?

11) Extra sets of keys

- to a Nissan (with a new muffler)
- to the now-dead minivan (suburban *de rigueur*)
- to my office building's elevator door (How many do I need?)
- to a Suzuki I junked a decade ago. I haven't completed Kübler-Ross's stages of grief yet.
- and a key fob that says "#1 DAD." I grew misty when my kids gave me this one Father's Day. "What's wrong?" Hope asked. "It's a very nice gift," I answered, but that's not the reason for the tears. I am not #1. I am not even #1 million in the Best Dad Competition. I have failed them in so many ways, grand and small. At times I feel like I'm doing okay; other times I feel they'd be better off with someone else to parent them. My wife knows what she's doing. Mostly I stand and watch and try not to screw the kids up.

12) My first mobile phone

When I bought the phone, I told my wife, "We'll only use it for emergencies." Oh, *yeah*. My friend Tom Buell calls this "the slippery slope of new technology."

13) Parking Ticket, City of Pittsburgh, Meter Violation, $15

I fail to put a quarter in, I get a $15 fine? That's a sixty-fold penalty! I'm filing a lawsuit. The parking police blatantly discriminate against those who park illegally. I can prove it. Class action, here I come.

14) The Words "Those Who Ignore Mystery Are Bound to Repeat It" Written on a Scrap of Paper

A parody of the line from George Santayana, who said, "Those who ignore history are bound to repeat it." It's the beginning of an essay I thought about writing. That's it. That's as far as I've gotten.

TRACK 3

Sixteen-and-a-Half Years Old

I engaged in all forms of stupidity—
sometimes aware, sometimes obtuse,
all beginning with the words why not?
uttered as if a dare.

Mostly it ended with *I'll tell you why not.*
The terrible toll of physics: Wheels not meant
for that kind of speed.
Centrifugal force outpacing the tepid friction of rubber
against an outsized curve.
Or the long night spent on the calculus of cause: a careless flick of a
purloined cigarette, and suddenly Mr. Monahan is standing in the
driveway with the other volunteer firemen,
talking to dad, looking at me,
bright lights flickering against his face,
a leaking hose trained on the newly blackened garage.

Yet there were moments when we escaped physics, no reason.
We'll shoot the rapids at Ohiopyle—no rafts! A gaggle of idiots,
screaming against the springtime sky. Then, like Paul on his horse,
we're
     falling
         falling,
struck from our bottomless mounts,
struck dumb with epiphany and regret:
Of course it must end like this, all waterlogged and desperate.
And stupid.

But then we emerge from beneath the frigid falls,
miraculous, all ragged cuts and hematomas,
veteran idiots with stories to tell,
survival, scars, wisdom, why not.

TRACK 4 › SEPTEMBER MORN

TRACK 4A

A Different Language

In early September 2001, I was asked to give a speech to the Homestead Free Library Association. Between the invitation and the day I gave the speech (September 22), some things happened...
Here is what I said that night.

I had a nifty speech prepared for tonight. I teach at Pitt, and September—not April—is the cruelest month for teachers. So, in an abnormal move for me, I finished the speech early. Before September 11. When I looked at it again—after last Tuesday—the speech seemed to be written in a different language, or, like the Apostles at Pentecost, I woke up and found myself speaking in a new and different tongue. Unfortunately, unlike the Apostles, my new tongue is not proclaiming good news. The language I now speak—the language we all speak—is the jargon of grief and retribution, tinged with a dialect of resignation, knowing that justice might come at the sacrifice of more blood, and we've already seen plenty of that.

So, I begin, awkwardly, with an apology. I ask you to bear with me as I struggle with my new tongue. What follows is a writer's mind in free-fall, trying to understand an unfamiliar vernacular, trying desperately to explain what this building and its books and its countless stories can mean in a suddenly unfamiliar world.

The first story begins on a September morning not too long ago. Daylight was misty until the sun burned off the fog and awoke Americans everywhere, including sleepy New Yorkers. But the sky was soon rent by explosions and smoke and confusion and endless agony. By the end of the day, 3,500 people lay dead, and not just New Yorkers. Thousands more were wounded, many mortally; thousands more were missing.

Several days later the president saw an opportunity in this tragedy, a chance to bring the nation together and forever change this course of the conflict and the nation. He spoke boldly of freedom and the cost of freedom, of the value inherent in the country's founding, and how Americans would not be in bondage to their fear. In fact, he said, no American would be in bondage, period. And so it was, on September 22, 1862—139 years ago today—Abraham Lincoln signed the Emancipation Proclamation, freeing southern slaves from the most horrid of human institutions.

The Union victory—if even history can call it a victory—that emboldened Lincoln to act was the battle of Antietam Creek in Maryland, whose waters, witnesses said, ran red that day. The 51st New York had fought that day—September 17, 1862—as did the 51st Pennsylvania and Americans from everywhere. It was the single bloodiest day in American history, with more total casualties than the War of 1812, the Mexican War, and Spanish American War combined. It represented the largest loss of life in a one-day conflict on American soil ever—until last Tuesday.

And so, a story, a revised perspective. Here's another wartime story about words and letters, on a somewhat lighter note: In 1941 my father worked at J&L Steel down the road, trying to get money to attend Pitt. My grandmother, fearing the coming conflict, wrote to President Roosevelt and asked that her only son, my father, be exempted from the draft. God only knows what my grandmother, possessor of an eighth-grade education, said in her letter, but it must have been persuasive because it worked: My father was exempted. No more fears about telegrams that read, "Greetings from your President."

My father, however, was not amused. When the war came, he enlisted, and thus became the subject of my grandmother's short-lived consternation, and subject of family lore forever.

Every family tells stories. Storytelling is what distinguishes us from other species. Think of it: Telling stories is the single thing that cleaves us from the rest of God's creatures. Consider your family's story—if it's anything like mine, your family's legends are so swamped with shared history that you can't separate fact from fiction. For example: What really happened is that your great great great Uncle Robert shook hands with Abe Lincoln's cousin; but by the time the story filters down to you, Uncle Bob is a hero who took one of Booth's bullets at Ford's Theatre. In my family, there's the vacation at Williamsburg where the car broke down seventeen times and my father, beside himself with misery, began to whistle hysterically; on another vacation at Ocean City, a beachcomber casually remarked to my parents that a two-year-old boy (that would be me) had fallen into a tidal pool and hadn't moved in a while. Who can tell, with the remove of so many years, what's real or not? What matters is the essence: the car that drove my father to near madness, or the vacation when I almost drowned. The rest is mere detail, colors to fill in the cartoon background.

And so these stories grow arms and legs and strut around our dinner conversations. As these stories age, they become clumsy and unwieldy, but we don't care, as long as they can fit in the room and keep us informed, keep us entertained. The goal isn't accuracy but to categorize family lore so that the story—the Big Story, the Story of Who We Are—can be told again and again. There is nothing inherently funny about my nearly drowning in Ocean City, but the story imparts a certain grace and redemption to those anxious moments when my father reached into the water and pulled me up, and I sputtered and coughed, back on dry land, back among the living, back with my family, full of stories to tell.

And here's one of the stories I like to tell: It's about Jeannette

Rankin. Show of hands: how many of you know who Jeannette Rankin is? Trust me, no one under the age of fifty has ever heard of her. She was famous for two things: she was the first woman in Congress—elected in 1916, when most states didn't allow women to vote, let alone run for office—and she was the only representative to vote against the United States' entry into both World War I and World War II. She was, in fact, the only member of Congress to vote against FDR's Declaration of War on December 8, 1941. For that single action she would be forever vilified. Later, at age eighty-seven, she would lead the Jeannette Rankin Brigade in a March on Washington to protest American involvement in the Vietnam War.

I mention her story for a single, important reason: Not because I am a great fan of Jeannette Rankin—though her life makes great material for a writer—but because I first read her story in a library. That probably doesn't surprise you, but many other people in many other parts of the world would be absolutely stunned to learn that I did. You see, in our country, we keep records of our history, our stories, even the unpopular ones. We allow books to circulate that are critical of America, of certain American principles, of who we are. Some books aren't just critical, but downright hostile, and you can find them in this library, today, right now. You can read books like *Lincoln Reconsidered,* or *Don't Know Much about the Civil War,* and find out that Abraham Lincoln wasn't exactly a paragon of virtue; that his decision about the Emancipation Proclamation had political aims as well as ethical ones.

We Americans accept all this without a second thought—that we are sitting in a building financed by Andrew Carnegie, housing books that are critical of Andrew Carnegie. We are sitting a stone's throw from the site of the Homestead Steel Strike, one of the most infamous battles in labor history, in a showdown between the Pinkertons and the steel workers almost 110 years ago. Witnesses say the water ran red that day too. And you can get an account of that battle from every conceivable angle—including those mighty critical of Carnegie—right here in this Carnegie Library, and no one will tell you what to think.

And if that isn't amazing enough—and, by God, don't you think it is?—and if that isn't amazing enough, all of this access to all of this knowledge will cost you no more than your tax dollar. No hidden charges. And if you're too poor to pay taxes, well, then—you get it all for free. And if you're underage, you still get it all for free. And if you don't have a home or you're from out of town, then you, too, can read for free or get on the Internet or read newspapers or encyclopedias or whatever you want. For free.

I'm sorry, but that's just crazy. Whatever one thinks of Andrew Carnegie, one must admit that he could have given his workers' communities their swimming pools and gymnasiums and just skipped all those incredibly dangerous books and their incredibly dangerous ideas and all those dangerous stories that make you think and reconsider and reorder your world. He did not.

And if that isn't crazy enough, sixty years ago some visionary folks got together and decided to be stewards to this insane concept, this free library. They would come together and do what they could, year in and year out, to keep this notion alive, to serve the communities' needs, to offer access to information and to help build the collection for even more stories, even more ideas. If that isn't proof that your organization's founders needed their collective heads examined, I don't know what is.

But it occurs to me that all of these stories—about Antietam, about Jeannette Rankin, about Andrew Carnegie—were already here, in this building, before September 11. Maybe I'm wrong. Maybe the language hasn't changed. Maybe the texts handed down from Virgil and Moses and St. Paul and Dante and Blake and Twain and Lincoln and Rankin all speak in the same tongue, the voice of human experience, the human story, where we find, as one writer said, that all our secrets are the same. Maybe a library—with all its amazing inconsistencies and wonderful records and memories—reflects the same strange diverse chorus that makes up who we are—ever changing, ever alive, ever curious.

A few last stories. On a September morning not too long ago, a group of people got together; some boarded planes and forever changed the landscape of New York, of Washington, of America. There were maybe four or five dozen people who engineered this feat that changed our history. There are that many people in this room right now. And on one of those planes were four or five folks who called home and found out that their plane was part of a much bigger plan, and that their destiny was being mapped for them. They didn't accept that. In the immortal words of one of those heroes, "We know we're going to die, and some of us are going to do something about it."

Someday, in the not too distant future, their stories will be here in this library for the next generation to read, thanks to the resources of the folks in this room right now. My wife the religious historian says that it's one way we define heroes: by the way we tell their stories over and over again.

Finally, a last reflection, by another Pittsburgh writer, Annie Dillard from her essay, "Total Eclipse." I end tonight the way I began, with a writer's struggle to communicate experience, with a writer's struggle to have words—to have all our words, all our stories—live on in places like this:

> All those things for which we have no words are lost. The mind—the culture—has two little tools, grammar and lexicon: a decorated sand bucket and matching shovel. With these we bluster around the continents to do all the world's work. With these we try to save our very lives.

Thank you very much.

TRACK 4B

I Love You in a Post-9/11 Way

My wife and I are in the middle of a fight. (Middle = she has yet to admit she's wrong.) Any couple who's been married for a while—even eight, nine months—won't be surprised that my wife and I are "having a discussion," as my sainted mother used to say. My kids, however, would be shocked. Once, when I picked them up after work, the babysitter said, "So I hear you and Sandee don't fight."

"Only one fight," I told her. "It started in 1983 and never quite stopped."

"Good," Karen said. She didn't want to be sitting for aliens.

It's inevitable: Marital artists are also martial artists. When people label divorce rates "shocking," I agree—I'm shocked they're not higher. I once asked Sandee's Great Uncle Jim what the secret was to his fifty-three years of marriage to Aunt Margaret. He replied, "The first fifty-two years are the hardest." I laughed, then stopped, because he wasn't laughing. It wasn't a joke.

I speak to you as a happily married man. (I can't speak for Sandee, because she's not speaking to me right now.) By every measure, my wife and I are good friends, compatible, in love, etc. But at times like these—rare, but there nonetheless—we have trouble being in the same zip code, let alone the same house. At some point, I know, we'll make up; but right now that point seems like a faint light through a telescope, a galaxy far, far away. Every couple has these skirmishes, but that provides scant comfort when you are in the trenches yourself. To paraphrase Tolstoy: Happy couples are all alike; each unhappy couple is unhappy in its own way.

But this fight is different. This fight started yesterday, another September 11 anniversary. As angry as I am, as convinced as I am that I'm right, I can't help but feel a little foolish.

I have a wife to argue with. There's a widow somewhere who would love one more chance to bicker with her husband.

My kids have both parents intact—married, divorced, happy, unhappy, fighting, cuddling, whatever, we're still here for them. We're still here, period.

And it's difficult to fight about—whatever it is that I'm right about—when a real fight is going on, with bullets and flak and collateral damage. I was thinking I could send Sandee a nice card—you know, a little Hallmark icebreaker that says *Sorry you're ticked; I'm still right*—but it's been so long that she might hesitate to open an envelope with strange handwriting and the wrong postage.

I shouldn't joke. Actually, like Great Uncle Jim, I'm not really joking. My wife and I should feel foolish for arguing. I know it's inevitable, I know every couple does it. I know that marriage is a challenge blah blah blah...but in the back of my mind, in the lockbox marked "forever," is the memory of those twin towers. I still see them standing there, wedded together, solid and sound, and then suddenly it's raining debris, nothing left but orphans and smoke, the occasional dog sniffing for signs of life. There was no warning; maybe we should have seen it coming. Maybe we took that skyline for granted, thinking that nothing could rend those two asunder, and then there you are, speechless in front of your children, trying to explain this new, unplanned topography, the one with the crater where the people used to be.

And I remember sensing that crater, 370 miles away yet right in my bedroom, and I remember pulling Sandee close and praying, praying, praying for all the long nights and hard questions that unique couples require, praying into the gathering autumn darkness for just one more chance to say *I'm sorry, I'm so sorry, I was so wrong.*

TRACK 5 > LIFE: A PRIMER

TRACK 5A

Sonograms

The first time was bizarre:
her swollen belly an enormous dinner roll glazed with jelly.
With each pass the image bobbed across the screen—
There's the liver, that's the heart...
You can tell she doesn't like this—see the frown on her face?

Your wife squeezed your hand: a little girl.

You knew you were looking at your nascent baby,
your *al dente* daughter,
but it could've been a map of Sweden,
the exotic geography of a foreign land
where everything was new
and anything was possible.

But this time the reason is as dark as the room.
The wand slithers across her flat stomach;
you hold your breath, trying to read each coy image,
trying to read the technician's face:
Is that a frown?
What's he see?
What's there that shouldn't be?

This isn't Sweden. It's Cossack Russia,
the Goths at the gates,
the Cambodia of Pol Pot.
Your wife's womb has been hijacked to another country,
and now fights the whim of a rogue junta
and its mechanized troops
spreading chaos into the streets

and you, too, have been drafted into battle—
a weaponless conscript hurling rocks at oncoming tanks.

You squeeze her hand.

It's OK, it's OK, it'll be fine, you say,
and turn headlong into the fire.

TRACK 5B

The LifeMeter

The Bible ciphers our lives at three score years plus ten. Turns out that's just a divine guesstimate—your mileage may vary. Now, thanks to my new, nearly-ready-for-prototype invention, the LifeMeter (patent pending), you'll know exactly how many steps you have left before you join the Choir Invisible.

The LifeMeter combines The Human Genome Project with algorithms developed by Google. By searching for the "kill switch" imbedded in each cell, LifeMeter calculates the magic tipping point when you'll go belly up. Advanced technology also permits LifeMeter to pinpoint the odds of real-time events and compare them to your unique skills. For instance, LifeMeter notes that there's an excellent chance your poor spatial skills will one day put you in touch with the 71D Hamilton—not so much on the bus as in front of the bus—and that day happens to be next Friday afternoon around 3:20 p.m.

But think of the advantages of such foresight:

Late for work? Hmmm, if you have fifty-three years and twenty-six days left, that whole employment thing is still useful. But if you know your liver isn't going to last the decade, then tell your boss you'll be in when you feel like it. Find a good trout stream instead. Couple more years and you won't be late for anything—you'll just be late.

Trouble at home? Check the gauge. If you'll be needing these folks to pick out your funeral suit soon, you should patch things up. But if your eulogy is eons away, then lay low. It'll blow over. Plenty of time to reconcile later—and it'll certainly wait until after the Pitt/ Notre Dame game.

Problems with that rebuilt transmission? Before you complain about the warranty, check your own—if both of you expire in six months, why worry?

Of course, the alternative, low-tech option would be to always live your life mindful and engaged, focused on friends and fulfillment and the world writ large. It's the kind of thing you think when someone dies: *Life is so short; I want to live my life as if I meant it.* But that's such a cliché, and who wants to be known as a Hallmark sympathy card? The LifeMeter is much easier. It takes away the mystery and ineffable nature of our existence, and gives us a digital readout of our allotment. Who *wouldn't* want such a handy tool? What would we do without it?

TRACK 5C

Note to New Users

Not all patients experience these side effects.
Chances are you will.

In clinical trials, some participants complained of headache,
nausea, cramping, chest pain, and constipation. That was Day
One. Others reported the shakes, the jitters, and the willies. Fewer
than the two percent complained of the heebie-jeebies or feeling
verklempt.

Some described a transient mix of torpor and hopelessness;
the rest just didn't care.

Some reported a decrease in sex drive,
but most blamed it on their fat spouse.

Insomnia was a big one—
staring into the long face of night, no end in sight.
Some sought relief by watching C-SPAN;
others made long-distance calls to old girlfriends,
with limited success.

Respondents indicated an increase
in depression and suicidal thoughts,
the very symptoms this drug was meant to cure.
Only ten percent noted the irony.

The use of alcohol is both
not recommended and widely reported.

If you experience any of these warning signs,
please talk with your health care provider
to decide whether these symptoms are authentic
or simply part of the human condition
and you hadn't noticed—
too numb to remember how suffering sleeps like Nero's lion,
only to be dragged daily from its cage just for sport.

The full effect of your medication won't be felt for four to six weeks.
By that time, you'll be back to your normal self.

The manufacturer cannot be responsible
for what that might entail.

TRACK 5D

Bury My Knee at Wounded Heart

My right knee used to be one of my better knees. No more. A year ago I was playing dek-hockey when a very large young man fell on it, and my anterior cruciate ligament snapped like a geriatric rubber band. I had surgery to replace the missing piece with a donation from a cadaver. (It's pretty bad when a dead guy's knee is in better shape than your own.)

Rehab was difficult. Tara, my physical therapist, was extraordinarily patient and encouraging, but she used the famous "we" voice found only in medicine. ("Why don't we try to do some more reps and work it out more?") And I thought to myself, "Who's *we*?" I found I could do many more leg extensions by visualizing that I was kicking Tara in the shin.

I learned a lot about myself during recovery—none of it good. I have the emotional maturity of a four-year-old, and that's indubitably unfair to most four-year-olds. I cannot wait, even when waiting is best; I cannot allow others to help, even if it means delaying my own recovery. Worse, I can be prickly and tense, especially to those I love.

There are times when I wonder whose knee ligament I received. The only thing I know about the donor is that he was male and under fifty—which makes his death all the more tragic. Yet here I sit a year later, not pain free but back to playing hockey, thanks to his family's generosity.

It's lucky I met the right medical criteria for his donation—the right blood type, the right gender. I'm glad they didn't ask for the right attitude—apparently I still have much, much more rehab to do on that front. The knee muscles have bounced back, but the pumping red muscle in my chest has become flabby and ineffective; I apparently need to do some more reps and work it out more.

TRACK 5E

Play-by-Playback

Sandee's cousin Carol got the news. The examination. The diagnosis. The long-term prognosis—sorry, the *lack* of long-term prognosis. The kind of news no one wants to hear, especially at twenty-three.

Always a practical woman, Carol arranged for a quick marriage to her boyfriend, Gary—a bizarre, hasty affair combining Jewish and Catholic wedding rites in an Episcopal chapel. Despite the urgency of the situation—or maybe because of it—we partied. We toasted. We danced. And then we went home and waited—our turn to get the news, to grip the phone hard, to find the right words of comfort in the face of someone dying so young, so suddenly.

Last week we got the call. Cousin Carol had passed away—twenty-five *years* after the original diagnosis, twenty-five years after that weird, weird, weird wedding.

She didn't beat the odds; she crushed the odds—but at a price. Radiation, a bone-marrow transplant (a gift from her brother), more radiation, surgery, endless chemotherapy, endless time in the hospital. And she was not a patient patient—she was never shy to tell you what she thought, even if perhaps you hadn't asked. For Carol, there was, quite literally, no time like the present. Fate had taught her not to wait for the right moment. Every moment is the right moment; every moment is now.

During the eulogy, Gary told us a story: a few days before she died, Carol had managed to score box seats to the sold-out season opener of her beloved Washington Nationals. No one made it to the game; we all met for her funeral instead. Looking at her casket, Gary said, "Somehow she still got the best seat."

It's true. She sits in the best seat in your heart—she and the others who have gone before us. She's the one telling you not to wait. She's the one telling you that odds are meant to be beaten. She's the one telling you to love hard. She's the one telling you to enjoy the game *now*.

Carol, it's summer now; the sun is out, I'm sitting in the left-field bleachers cheering a come-from-behind win because by God that's why we're here.

TRACK 6

In the Express Lane

So I'm trying to decide
if my dozen asparagus count as one item or twelve
(the guy behind me with the eye patch and the bok choy definitely
thinks
I'm in the wrong line)
and I'm trying to remember which gum four out of five dentists
recommend
and wonder what the deal is with the fifth dentist
when I see the headline
BRITNEY SPEARS CAUGHT SMOKING ON THE BALCONY
and I start imagining that poor girl
smoldering on the veranda
and, underneath, the headline
POP STAR'S PASTOR SAYS CIGARETTES NOT CHRISTIAN
and just when I start to wonder if breast implants
and midriff tops are
theologically okey-dokey

the one-eyed guy nudges the back of my legs with his cart
and the cashier asks if I'm going to buy that or just read it
but my mind is all atitter now with images of this
newly chested girl aglow on the balcony like a crop-topped hibachi
and I think oh please please please please please
will somebody just put Britney out please

(with apologies to Frank O'Hara)

TRACK 7

Letter to My Daughter

Gracie,

I'm sorry. I screwed up.

When you asked me why your friend Suzanne killed herself, I said "Don't ask why, hon. It won't get you anywhere."

At first I thought it was a good answer—it avoided clichés, and you hate clichés. Besides, you knew Suzanne; her act was so out of character that clichés wouldn't work. And it's a painfully honest answer, because you'd see through a lie. You always do.

That answer is born out of experience. People ask that question all the time—why would a beautiful, popular college sophomore end her life? Why was your Aunt Cindy paralyzed in a sledding accident? Why can't your cousin Liza catch a break?

No one knows. So why ask why? Besides, what if Suzanne had left a note that said, "I'm going to kill myself because…" what answer would make sense? What answer would *be* an answer, instead of just leading to more questions?

But that's not why I said what I said. I said it because I'm as scared and confused as you are. A question like that means you're questioning your faith—what kind of loving God would let something like this happen? (I know, because I'm asking myself the same thing.) Then I worry that the question becomes a slippery slope: if you can't find an answer to why, maybe you start thinking Suzanne was on to something, and I cannot cannot cannot bear that thought.

But I was wrong. Go ahead and ask why. It may be useless, but you want to know because you're searching for meaning. When you were a kid, I could've come up with something; now you're on your own search, and I can't stop you. I shouldn't have tried to stop you.

I do know this: Suzanne fired one shot, and that bullet ripped through several hundred people. Look around at the funeral tomorrow; count the wounded. They'll be easy to spot. Suzanne loved her family, so I can only guess she wasn't herself when she picked up that gun. When you remember her, remember her running around the beach, possibly the worst volleyball player ever. Remember her inordinate fondness for butternut squash. Remember how she'd revel in thunderstorms.

And remember what Jesus did when told of Lazarus' death: "Jesus wept." It's the shortest, most powerful verse in the New Testament. Everyone knows the story of raising Lazarus, but we forget that moment when his best friend broke down and cried. There was no looking up to heaven asking why. There was no pretense, there were no clichés, no *he's in a better place*. Just two words: Jesus wept. Before you turn your back on the divine—as Christ is my witness, I would not blame you—remember that being human (even the true God and true man variety) means suffering and sadness and loss... and friendship and love and forgiveness. And thunderstorms and volleyball and butternut squash. All of these, all at once.

If you're asking why, that means you're confused because you loved Suzanne more than she loved herself. It shows you're a sensitive, compassionate, wonderful friend. It shows you're alive. If Suzanne couldn't see that in herself, then we have to see it for her. That will be your *mitzvah*: living your life because Suzanne can't live hers—in this world—anymore. Maybe the question of why will be forever on your lips, and that's okay. Like every father, I want to be there for you for the rest of my life, to answer your questions, to hold you when you're crying, to tell you everything will be all right.

It won't.

But it will. And don't ask why I know these things. I just do.

Love, always,

Dad

TRACK 8 > ONLY SHADES OF GRAY

TRACK 8A

Some Dyed for Beauty

I was 33 when I first heard
You're looking distinguished.
I think of Jesus—were his temples turning gray?
Is that what caused the ruckus? The overturned tables?

The drugstore boxes promise
youthful brunette in five minutes.
If I wait ten, could I go back to high school?
Would girls speak to me this time?
Can I assure them a tall, dark, confident future,
instead of this retreating crown of white thorns,
this colorless mane of middle age?

I skip the watery Grecian Formula and
turn to a heady, full-bodied Chablis.
If the cashier asks for my ID,
I will lean my weathered face forward and
kiss her full on the lips.

TRACK 8B

The Color of Forgiveness

So I went to a new place to get my haircut. (I have exacting standards for my barber: Are they cheap? Are they close by? Are they open?) The stylist greeted me with clipboard in hand. She had a few questions, among them: *Do you blow-dry your hair?* (Once, I think—for the prom.) *Do you use oil or gel?* (Oil. Quaker State. 5W-30. Oh, you mean on my scalp?) And the kicker: *Do you dye your hair?*

I looked at her. My hair is nearly all white. Do I dye my hair? Yes. Yes, I do. I *chose* this color. I go to the drug store and look through all the possible variations, and I pick the box labeled Premature Gray. What was she thinking?

I'm very good at recognizing dumb things people say because I'm very good at saying dumb things. Ironically, I'm not so good at forgiving others their imperfect moments.

That's why Peter is my favorite apostle. This guy was thick with a capital I. When Moses and Elijah appear out of nowhere beside Jesus, Peter suggests that they build a nice little hut for each of the three of them—"for he did not know what to say," Matthew notes.

Apparently not. His boss is transfigured before him, with great prophets rampant, and Peter pipes up with the first thing that springs to mind: real estate! It would have been better, of course, if he had simply enjoyed the moment. But Peter is too human for that.

You gotta love the guy. Luckily, someone did. Someone saw something in the fisherman that no one else saw, and a church began. The premise was simple, and simply outrageous: You're forgiven for the dumb things you say, as long as you love your neighbor— even the gray-haired one, so quick to judge, so slow to forgive, who needs much more than dye to hide his many human imperfections.

TRACK 8C

My Goodness, You're Good-Looking

The hot dog vendor near my office is a friend of mine. He dispenses kielbasa and unsolicited advice in equal measures. I was walking near his stand recently; ahead of me was a woman with an extremely short, military-style buzz cut.

"Hey," the vendor said, "nice hair style."

She shot him an absolutely withering look, then picked up her pace.

The vendor looked at me, arms out. "I was serious," he pleaded.

For some stupid reason, I felt compelled to make things right. I caught up with the woman. "Look," I said. "He's a good guy. He meant it as a compliment."

She said nothing for a moment, and I figured I had just compounded the problem. I was about to peel off in another direction and save what little face I had left—then she spoke.

"It's not a 'style,' " she said. "It's chemotherapy, and it's not nice."

Now it was my turn to say nothing. A thousand thoughts went through my head, and I'm embarrassed to say that the first one was, *how did I get myself into this?* But it wasn't about me, or anything to do with me. I decided to speak the truth, because this woman had no doubt exhausted her patience with lies—little ones, big ones, the whole lie family.

"I think it looks nice, too," I said. "Seriously. I can't explain why—it just does."

More silence. We were used to silence by now.

"Thanks," she said finally. "I don't see how it's possible, but thanks." And we parted without another word.

I won't—I *can't*—pretend to know what that woman had gone

through, is going through. She assumed the loss of her once-long locks was symptomatic of a more massive loss. But you can't fool hot dog vendors. No no no. They know the real you. A thousand people a day parade past, but they know the truth about you: My goodness, you're good looking. My goodness, you've got style.

TRACK 9

Giving Back What I Lent

Quick quiz: Who said which of the following—Jesus or Kim Kardashian?

> *"I'm so annoyed I dyed my hair dark! ...[I] wanted a fresh look. BUT now I am missing my light hair! HELP!!! What do I do?"*

> *"Consider the lilies of the field, how they grow; they toil not, neither do they spin: And yet I say unto you, that even Solomon in all his glory was not arrayed like one of these."*

I know—tough call. Turns out Choice A wasn't Jesus. But here's the kicker: for all the stone-cold crazy that comes from Kimmie's mouth, Our Lord's own *bon mots* were also off the tracks. "Give to the poor" this and "don't cast the first stone" that. Nutty, nutty stuff.

Usually I give up two things for Lent—fresh lobster and good intentions. But this year I'm trying a new game:

I'm gonna live like Jesus.

No, no—no seamless tunics, or even unseemly tunics. No healing the sick—though if I could, I'd start with the clutch on my Mazda. No sitting at the right hand of God, or any other almighty limb. No. I'm going to try (add extraordinary emphasis on *try*) to focus on the same things Jesus focused on.

If you want to play at home, here are the rules of the game—which I'm making up right now:

- Any approach you follow has to come from Matthew, Mark or Luke. (John's gospel plays by different rules that many of us find hard to cipher.)

- Don't focus on the heavenly kingdom, the messianic or the miraculous. Those things are way outside your pay grade. Despite what your mom thought, you are *not* the Second Coming.

- Pay attention to the preaching—but don't preach yourself. No one wants to hear you pontificate around the water cooler, *Verily I say unto you...*

- Exclude the Passion and the Resurrection—for now. There will be plenty of colored eggs later. (You also might want to skip the overturning-the-tables-at-the-temple part...Mrs. Darini just spent a lot of time setting them up for next week's rummage sale.)

So what's left? We're left with the Jesus of the everyday. That's the Jesus I suggest we try to copy for forty days of the year. The Jesus who rests when he's tired, who doesn't ignore the hungry, who shows compassion for widows and orphans and prisoners. The Jesus who thinks you should turn the other cheek—even if it's the guy who just cut you off fifty feet from the exit, and he totally saw you. The Jesus who's simple enough to ask Our Father only for daily bread, but can still accept a gift of oil to anoint himself after a tough day. The Jesus who—like the rest of us—wrestles with demons. The Jesus who could've turned water into grape juice, but wants to keep the wedding party going so he breaks out the good stuff. The Jesus whose political message is a single phrase: give Caesar what is Caesar's and give God what is God's. And then there's the easier-for-a-camel-to-pass-through-the-eye-of-a-needle-than-a-rich-man-to-enter-heaven thing…huh? That's…well…that might be tough to explain to the mortgage company. Maybe I can pay ahead.

Maybe I'll try loving my neighbor by helping to load her cart at the supermarket, instead of secretly seething because she has way more than twelve items in the express lane. And instead of trying a new rice-and-green-tea diet (endorsed by Kimmie, no doubt), maybe I'll send some money to people whose diet is exclusively rice and green tea—and not nearly enough of either. Instead of worrying about work, maybe I'll work on not worrying.

What happens when you leave first-world problems behind and focus on what's left? I don't know, but I guess I'll find out. Maybe I'll report on my progress, keep a blog, post it on Facebook…

…but then there's this story about giving alms—how the right hand should not know what the left hand is doing…

See what I mean? Nutty, nutty stuff. Thank God Lent is only forty days.

TRACK 10 > TEACHABLE MOMENTS

TRACK 10A

Daddy's Little Girl Scout Camp

I just returned from Girl Scout Camp. Please—no comments. I've heard them all—everything from "I'll bet you look good in a Girl Scout uniform" to "My Daddy thinks you're crazy for coming here." I smile weakly. Dads are always right.

Truth is, I've come back with a new appreciation of Girl Scouts. I use the word "appreciation" in every sense, as in *gratitude* and *I appreciate how painful a root canal can be*. For those of you who have young daughters, here is a report from the trenches.

• **Little girls have two volumes: loud and jarring.** A few girls talking together sound like rabid Chihuahuas on crack; twelve girls talking together constitute an OSHA violation.

Now, this is not always true. Girls whisper a lot, usually after passing through the "Gates of Silence" at the flag ceremony each day. I saw one girl cup her hand and whisper to another. A leader leaned down and told her to be quiet; the girl nodded and cupped *both* hands over her friend's ear. The leader sighed and let it go. I appreciate that.

• **Dr. Spock was wrong: Kids don't need sleep.** Of course, sleep is an excellent idea, but these girls saw it as an optional activity, like flossing. By my count, their eyes were closed for 12.7 minutes a night, rarely at the same time. Then again, we made sure we wired our charges with chocolate s'mores, each of which contains 983 percent of your daily sugar requirement. What a smart bedtime snack for jacked-up little girls.

• **Karl Marx was on to something.** At camp everyone takes turns at everything. That's *everyone*, including camp leaders. At the end of group meals, each table drew straws to determine "kapers"—dishwasher, dryer, table cleaner. Twice I drew dish duty—"Bubbler I." One mom took a picture—"I'll send it to your wife," she offered. I smiled weakly.

Everyone sings at camp, at every opportunity, most often in a chain-gang chant. I don't know if it was my Y-chromosome or too many s'mores, but I couldn't catch on. "Don't you know any songs, Mr. Collins?" For some perverse reason, I could only think of Lou Reed: "Hey babe, take a walk on the wild side...Hey sugar, take a walk on the wild side..." C'mon, everybody sing. I found the wisdom to keep that tune to myself.

Despite the commune-like work detail, ever-fluid cliques and in-groups pervade. This is painful for me, remembering my own run-ins with capricious popularity. I was tempted to intervene ("Next time Mary says your braids look ugly, tell her that her haircut makes her look like a rabid Chihuahua on crack.") but the truth is I could no more stop such stinging banter than I could wish away clouds. It's really a lesson for me *and* my kids: Take only compliments from peers, and good advice; ignore everything else they say.

• **Girls rule—if you give them a chance.** The troop went on the "Adventure Trail"—an obstacle course in the middle of the woods. Mostly the girls were game, but some were too quick to say those two dreaded words, "I can't." One obstacle was a ten-foot-high solid fence, requiring a rope, arm strength, and tenacity. After much cajoling from me and other adults, they lifted their heads of braided hair over the top. The look of happiness and surprise on each face made the whole trip worthwhile. SweetGodAlmighty, what a moment.

• **Girls can shop.** Go ahead, criticize the stereotype, but you weren't waiting for twelve girls to pick out a few dollars' worth of souvenirs at a Trading Post with the approximate square footage of a VW bus. One hour and twenty-five minutes. I spent less time picking out my last car.

• **Girl Scouts produce strong, independent women—but must we do it all at the same time?** Couldn't we take turns? Think of one fearless, assertive personality—asking questions, jostling for position, making her point. Now think of twelve such personalities in simultaneous expression. Do the math.

For Ashleigh and Missy, for Abby and Kaitlyn and Jordan and Katie, for Anna and Sarah and Jessica, and for my own strong, independent scouts, Faith, Hope and Grace—here is my camp song for you, sung in the baritone, off-key voice of a Girl Scout Dad: There are obstacles outside of camp, too, but it makes no difference because you can conquer any of them. I've seen you. You cannot imagine how glorious you look as you pull yourself upward, *willing* yourself to the next step, until I see your braided head arise, and I see that expression on your face.

I have one wish for your dreams, girls (provided, of course, that you ever go to sleep): May you see that look of surprised success in the mirror every blessed day of your sweet, limitless lives.

Now go to sleep. I mean it.

TRACK 10B

Solving for Why

Your seventh-grader looks up from her page of struggle and says
when will I ever need to know this?

She's right, of course.
The only graph that matters is actuarial:
birth, slope, death.
Tell her that.

Tell her to sleep through trig and wake up for literature,
unless it's Faulkner, then do the reverse.

Tell her to fall to her knees in science,
to be different,
to be Galileo for a day,
to feel the hot eyes of the not-different, the half-dead.

Tell her to re-live history in real time,
to sketch all maps to scale: one inch = one inch.

Tell her to stay away from guys with red hair.
They're trouble.
And while you're at it, from red-haired girls too.
Especially redheads named Tina—
Tina Celeste, for instance, of 121 Rawson Avenue,
who promised so much
who left you all cummerbunded and boutonnièred
one May evening
with nothing more than a story you had to suture to make funny.

Tell her to stay away from people
particularly people who don't smile at irony, no matter how black,
who find nothing thrilling in good scotch
who find nothing thrilling in bad scotch
who end up with a spouse named Tina with red hair,
bitter, rankled, half-dead with regret.

Tell her that prophets have losses.
That hiding from sorrow means finding it.
That the slope of life is always uphill yet accelerates against gravity
until one day you wake up screaming, shocked at the speed,
plunging into the chasm beyond the axis,
past the little arrow pointing to the right—
headlong into infinity.

You won't tell her any of this, of course.
It's her homework
not yours.

TRACK 10C

Open Letter to Pitt Students

Several years back, my employer, the University of Pittsburgh, suffered through scores of bomb threats. I was asked to give the opening remarks to Pitt's Student Sustainability Symposium during the last week of classes. In an ironic twist, the symposium itself had to be relocated because of a bomb threat. It presented, as they say, a teachable moment.

I'm sorry I'll miss so many of you before you leave campus for summer break. Instead of the usual sudden departure at the end of the term, it seems that our camp will break up in stages, as your parents pack you up rather than have you stand outside your dorm in the middle of the night, waiting for the police dogs to sniff the "all clear." Believe me, I understand.

I'm reminded of the Chinese curse, "May you live in interesting times." We've received eighty or ninety bomb threats in the final few weeks, disrupting classes, disrupting research, disrupting lives. True story: I received so many email notifications about bombs that my mail system routed anything marked "threat" to my spam folder.

When you think about it, "bomb threat" is a strange phrase. It's not a bomb; it's the *threat* of a bomb. As you know from physics class, bombs are concentrated packages of potential energy, full of heat and light. In another context, a concentrated form of potential energy wouldn't be a bad thing.

"Threat" is the problem. You never know how real it is. And that leads to a choice. You can take the threat seriously and take action, or you can ignore the threat and accept both the risk and the consequences. It's easy to get jaded and lazy and do nothing. Sure the Lord sitteth at the right hand of the Almighty, but entropy sitteth on the right hand of the couch, clutching the remote.

Here's the thing about inaction: It's an active choice too. Saying "no" to something means saying "yes" to something else, saying yes to consequences that will happen without you, maybe *because* of your absence. And your future is full of threats, as well as full of people who say there is no threat, that it can't be proven. And who wants to tangle with that level of uncertainty? Why bother?

Proof? Let me provide an example drawn from your political science class: Which is the most potentially powerful voting bloc in this country? Unions? Senior Citizens? Nope—it's the people who don't vote. Imagine if they got off the couch all at once and went to the polls. What would happen? No one knows, but it would change everything. Talk about unleashing potential energy.

The most powerful bomb in the world is inaction. It's ignoring threats because we don't understand them. That's the price you pay for developing a trained mind: You are required to do something; nihilism and dithering are no longer options.

At the risk of morphing into a physics lesson, how do you meet a force like that, a force so bent on vague and random threats? Turns out it's you. You're the answer. Turns out we're all concentrated forms of potential energy, waiting to release our light. Ironic, isn't it? Whoever made these threats promised to unleash energy on us, and it's frightening because we're afraid of what it might hold, how it might change our landscape. Yet isn't that why you're in college, trying to understand concepts such as energy and power, learning to divine fact from fiction, to distill truth from history? Instead of vague and random and terrifying, your work focuses and sharpens and refines knowledge, moves scholarship forward, raises rather than intimidates consciousness. Aren't you, too, anxious to generate the power to change the landscape forever?

Good for you. Good for us. Maybe that's the best revenge.

TRACK 10D

Note to My Daughter's Social Studies Teacher

Please excuse Hope's essay on the Boxer Rebellion,
which did not happen in 1066.
Sorry. I told her it did.
Age has gnawed away the meat of my memory,
leaving tiny crumbs that are ferried about by even tinier ants
who struggle to carry things ten times their weight.
Ants, as you know, are arachnids or nematodes or something,
I forget.
Anyway, the Norman Conquest was 1066.
I also remember Norman Lear, Norman Bates, and Norm Cash,
who once batted .361 for the Tigers, in case you're curious.

My brain is now a perverse rucksack of randomness—
phone numbers that begin with letters,
the firing order of my brother's Buick,
German articles in the dative case.
If we knew each other better, Miss Hoffman,
I could sing "Werewolves of London"
in its entirety, perhaps a bad idea.

Memory is a sordid mistress, Nietzsche said,
or maybe it was Jesus, who knows?
I can't say I've missed what I've lost, not that I could tell.
I remember my mother reading *Wynken, Blynken, and Nod,*
licking her finger as she turned each page.
The smell of a ginkgo seed I crushed underfoot
on my first day of college.

The taste of Sandee's earlobe after a run.
The surprising weight of a three-legged cat who used to sleep on
my chest.
No idea where my car is parked, but
total recall of Hope's first steps—footie pajamas and toothless grin,
arms like Frankenstein, falling forward into Sandee's lap,
another conquest
another lesson
another question
another day
until they pile up and tailgate each other and then
I can't remember why the Chinese rebelled,
perhaps driven mad by the scent of ginkgo
following them like Frankenstein into the crowd of history.

TRACK 10E

My Speech to the Graduates

(Editor's note: Mark Collins has patiently waited for his alma mater, the University of Pittsburgh, to invite him back as a commencement speaker. Each year he is snubbed in favor of someone "more accomplished" or "famous" or "lacking a criminal record." He's now decided to share his wisdom without the benefit of a formal invitation.)

Thank you, Chancellor, for that kind introduction. It sounded much better than when I scribbled it down half an hour ago.

In the interest of time and to justify my unvouchered lunch, allow me to offer a series of rousing plaudits along with equally rousing rebuttal. This is my generic stump speech, the equivalent of the anticipated mass in the Catholic Church: If you have an obligatory graduation to attend this spring, there's no need to go. You're already covered.

Let's get the ball rolling with the most common commencement address cliché:

The word commencement means "beginning," not an end. Every graduation speaker feels an obligation to mention that. If you don't know what the word "commence" means, perhaps those seven years of college have been misspent. Ironically, your student loan payments will, indeed, commence. The first bill is now waiting for you at home. That's the last efficient service you will ever receive from the financial services industry.

Ladies and gentlemen, we are at a crossroads where yesterday meets tomorrow. Frankly, I'd like to change this tired paradigm. I'd prefer if our crossroads were, say, 1981 and Apple was selling at $5 a share. Or I'd settle for last week, when I still had a working transmission. But no. We speak thoughtfully of "living in the moment" as if we had options. We're stuck here. We can try to bring hope to the hopeless, but after that it gets dicey. We can't bring list to the listless or feck to the feckless, so we do the best we can.

Remember to thank your parents, without whom you wouldn't be here. From where I stand, I can see your parents, and, much like you, I'd rather not imagine how you got here.

Don't forget where you came from. Ha! As if you could. I guess the idea is to keep you humble, but if anyone here has ever been in a family or knows of a family, then you know humiliation—sorry, humility. By the way, if any of you plan to find the cure for cancer just to prove your critics wrong, just to say I-told-you-so, feel free. Go ahead. Okel-dokel by me.

You are the future. This is my favorite graduation-day bromide. It gets all of us off the hook—*you're* not responsible for anything up till now because you're just graduating, even though you're twenty-two years old and can vote and drink and go off to war and get shot at, and *we're* not responsible for anything that happens after next week 'cause it's now up to you. Hate to burst everyone's bubble, but we're *all* citizens. We're all responsible for each other.

So are you getting cynical yet? Good, because that's my graduation gift to you. College is the last opportunity you have to be truly cynical. You can—you should—be suspicious, wary, guarded. That's a mark of intelligence. But cynicism is a luxury you can afford no longer. Ditto with the word promise, that hallmark of commencement speeches. It's time to produce. Do what you need to do, but don't do it for our sake. Don't do it for the sake of your family or this institution. Do it because you're a sentient being on this planet, third rock from the sun, alive among the living. It's the rarest of gifts. It's the fiercest of responsibilities. That's why we're all pulling for you. We want for you what we pray for ourselves: A chance. Another breath. *This* moment.

Aren't you curious why you're all dressed in flowing robes and funny hats? Because today you're all the same. I can't detect any differences among you. The next time you'll be treated so democratically is when you die. So somewhere between now and then, you have choices to make, places to go, things to accomplish. So don't be cynics. Be free. Be alive.

Now if someone can just validate my parking ticket, I'll leave the two of you—that is, you and your future—to work out the niggling details.

To My Daughters on Their Birthdays in Lieu of Gifts

When the first fish flopped onto the ancient sand,
sucking in the searing air,
there were no lifeguards,
no diving boards, no snack shop,
no chlorine in the primordial muck—which explains how we got
your cousin Larry.
Here is where you learn life, at water's edge.
Not language. Not words.
Words are born liars.
Lesson One: irony.

It stings to dive in,
where you and mosquitoes and 10,000 peers
compete for each square foot,
where you thrash and kick and learn no style but survival,
where you're stripped to your two-piece,
as close to Eden as the law allows.

Here is where you'll find what you came looking for,
not language, not words.
Words can't take the sun;
words have packed their ratty towels and gaudy suits and left.
And now you're left, too, without speech.
No one hears you beneath the surface.
No one hears if the same life-giving water
fills your little lungs and sends you to the bottom.
An alert guard might spy your shadow in the deep end, maybe not.
Would you have it any other way? Could you?

Mark Collins / 69

Life is lucky that way.
Life is laughter as you mug your sister.
Life is the unseen shadow.
Life is the mosquito.
Life is the first gasping fish—let's call him Skip—
bellying onto shore, just to see what's up.

This is all I have for you.
And sunscreen.
And my last name.
And irony.
And the taste of salt from some water nearby.

With apologies to Gerald Stern

TRACK 11 > HOW STILL WE SEE THEE LIE, AND LIE AGAIN

TRACK 11A

The Advent of Customer Service

Here's a story of a college sophomore earning some extra money by working at Home Depot. Her main complaint: guys trying to get her phone number, asking her out on dates—completely oblivious to the fact that she was (1) at work, (b) had no interest in them, and (iii) was some guy's daughter.

Specifically my daughter. "I can't believe it," she'd tell me. "It's 7 a.m., I'm wearing an ugly orange apron, and they're still hitting on me!"

Oh, honey, what you don't know about men and will have to learn.

But there's a larger point: It's part of the social fabric to complain about lousy customer service...yet never think that the problem could be us.

I know. I'm guilty myself. Once, after a particularly bad day, I stopped at Giant Eagle for a six-pack. (Yes, there's now beer at my local grocery store. In Pennsylvania, this is big, big news, but this revolution will not be televised.) The busy cashier overcharged me by forty-five cents. I was almost to my car when I realized her mistake, and stormed right back to demand my money. Oh, good for me. Did I really think it was a plot and not a mistake? *Let's see—forty-five cents here, forty-five cents there, and pretty soon I'll have...ninety cents!* Yessir. So glad I stopped her evil plan.

I realize that we all have stories of bad customer service. A few years back, I switched cable companies. I called the original cable company to find out where I should return their box; this turned into fifteen minutes of me defending my decision. "Are you sure? I can't believe that you're switching. You know, sometimes that other cable connection will suddenly go off...." The call ended shortly after I suddenly went off.

Stories like that seem legion. Actually, they're not. They're the exception. Did your lights come on today? Was your garbage picked up? Did the mail come? When you went to the gas station, was there gasoline available? Was your morning coffee served to you in a cup, or poured into your hands? Truth is, the overwhelming majority of business transactions happen without a hitch (and often without a thank you from us), and we don't think twice of the people who made that possible. I'm sorry your street wasn't salted last week, but the spreader jammed and Mike (remember Mike? Your neighbor Stash's oldest kid?) got up at 4 a.m. to fix it and had to order parts. It's too bad your trip to Denver was delayed for thirty-six minutes, but it seems unlikely that berating the flight attendant will increase the cruising speed of a 747. While we're at it, complaining about a 1,300-mile trip that takes four hours and fifteen minutes rather than three hours and forty minutes is just, well, foolish. "Oh, my flight was very bad..." In the words of comedian Louis CK, "Oh no it very wasn't." You just flew safely through the air in a metal can at 550 miles an hour. *Ponder* that. I'll wait.

Besides, I'm writing this during Advent for God's sake (literally). There may not be room at the inn, but surely there's room in your heart to cut that poor girl a break—the cashier with the orange apron who overcharged you forty-five cents because she's busy and slightly flustered by the long line of customers who are expecting so, so, so much: the stuff we take for granted every day. Besides, the customer in front of you just hit on her.

Instead, celebrate. Celebrate that you're here, alive during this magical time, that you've got so much stuff, that you've got both time and freedom to complain, that you can go across the street to ten other stores. Celebrate the fact that you're buying Uncle Stan a Christmas present that he really doesn't deserve because deep in your heart of hearts you know none of us do and maybe we should all start to act accordingly.

Holiday Email Apologia #37

Hi, Everybody,

Hope you're all misbehaving. I myself can be accused of many naughty things this year; I can't list them here, because I'm limited to 10.0 gigabytes per email. But I can't be accused of ingratitude. I know how blessed I am. It's apparent in so many ways—not the least of which is our enduring friendship, despite my spotty correspondence. So why is it that thankfulness feels so far away this year? I feel like a little kid at the dinner table, and my mom is telling me to eat all my food because there are starving kids somewhere, and I'm thinking, "We could send the Brussels sprouts to them—just give me their address and I'll help you pack it all up." What is *wrong* with me?

I dunno. The past year has proven that illness and suffering can show up uninvited, and you can't stop them from sitting on your couch and drinking all the good scotch. Yelling at them doesn't help; feigning sleep doesn't, either. I've spent the last year in varying stages of slouch, and (literally) my shoulders hurt.

But I have discovered two things: One, I have friends to whom I can send emails with lines like "What is *wrong* with me?" and they'll continue to read, which is amazing and I'm not kidding. There is no good reason to stick by me when I'm in such a black mood (the day before the day before Christmas!), yet you're *still* reading. I get slightly (i.e., still mannishly) teary-eyed thinking about that, and wonder what in God's name I've done to deserve such grace.

Much of my funk results from too much death and too much hospital, both really and virtually. Sandee's father passed; my sister is still sick; my aunt broke both hips (the latter one last week), and now a good friend of mine suffered a double mastectomy, which would be horrible news in any case…made worse by her husband's diagnosis of multiple myeloma not six months ago. It's almost too much to bear. I've been praying a lot, which leads me to the end of this sermon:

This year has been a learning experience (not a welcome learning experience, mind you, but a learning experience nonetheless). When friends and family are suffering (mental, physical, existential, whatever), I try to battle through the mundane details of my life, but it feels so unimportant. I'm aware, of course, that my students feel as if their college careers are of paramount importance, and (to them) they are. I have a student who's pregnant, a student who's considering dropping out of school (and, I think, blames me), and one who's so unsure about what classes to take, that she's driving me absolutely batty. We meet for thirty minutes at a time. After much kvetching and expressions of angst, she registers for one class. We're up to three now. Yesterday she asked me when she'll be able to graduate. It took a great deal of effort not to say, "At this rate, never."

But the truth is, I slog through, complaining about the weather, about my job, about my life—and then I think about my sister, my aunt, whomever, and suddenly I understand context. I understand the power of prayer. Anytime you pray for someone, you gotta wonder about the efficacy. And why do we recruit others to help? ("Listen, if you get a chance, could you pray for…") Here's why prayer works: for one moment, a singular moment, we bow our heads or bang our Buddhist cymbals or whatever, and we think about something other than ourselves. We send unselfish good wishes, for no reason at all. We get nothing out of it; we know there are no guarantees. And yet we do it; we take ourselves out of our selves and pray for someone we've never met—all because someone made a simple, humble request. Most of the folks praying for my sister or my friend with breast cancer—at Ralph's synagogue, for instance (Hi, Ralph!)—don't even know me. If the power of prayer comes down to this—a bunch of strangers with bowed heads, thinking about something Other—then it's worth it. The universe is a better place because of it. Does it make my sister feel less alone? I can't answer that. I *can* say it's pebbles in a pond—you never know how far the resulting waves might reach. And now I'm telling you all of this, because after many years I still think about you and understand context; I know which wave belongs to you and how it keeps me afloat, and I'm so very, very, very, very grateful.

> Merry Christmas, Happy Hanukkah,
> Happy Whatever Brings *You* Joy this season,
> Mark

TRACK 11C

Stocking Stuffed Full of It

Woe unto you, scribes and Pharisees, hypocrites! for ye pay tithe of mint and anise and cummin, and have omitted the weightier [matters] of the law, judgment, mercy, and faith: these ought ye to have done, and not to leave the other undone. [Ye] blind guides, which strain at a gnat, and swallow a camel.

Matthew 23:23-24

I live my life on parallel tracks. I spend summers on a motor scooter, saving on gas and saving the environment—and spend winters driving a 14-MPG pickup because I simply cannot let it go.

I spend my days proffering advice to undergraduates, suggesting well-planned classes and proper preparation for a career—advice that I have never, ever, ever followed.

Like any good parent, I set rules for my three daughters—the very rules I so skillfully ignored four decades ago.

One could argue that it's human nature, I suppose. Still, I'm surprised hypocrisy didn't make the list of seven deadly sins. (I'll bet it's eighth and closing fast.) Anger, lust, pride—at least you can *understand* those transgressions. Hypocrisy has this added gem: arrogance. *(Here's what you ought to do—trust me, I know better. Meanwhile I have no intention of doing anything like that.)*

Maybe that's what rankled Jesus. He seemed to hold special wrath for those who were full of high sentence but no real commitment. Unlike avarice or sloth, hypocrisy can sound so good: it has the smell and taste of solid advice, an experienced voice, wise counsel. In reality, it's a dressed-up hoax, and fancy lie—no matter how well-intended.

"We have met the enemy, and he is us," Walt Kelly's Pogo once said. Every year at Christmas we send the usual passel of clichéd holiday cards—*we really should get together...miss you so much*—but we never follow-through. The road away from God is paved with good intentions and no more, as if we have no more to offer. Like prayer. Like service. Like ourselves.

Whatever you have wrapped under the tree this year, may it be wrapped in humility and grace and honesty, the 13th, 14th, and 15th days of Christmas. They're far more rare than frankincense and myrrh, but with this single caveat: they're fragile. They can be so easily broken.

TRACK 11D

"And He Shall Be Called..."

I received a Christmas email update from a friend of mine living in Boston. It has not been a good year for Beth—her father died from cancer, she broke up with her boyfriend, and just found out she's pregnant.

This is ironic, because Beth is deeply religious. But she didn't use the word *ironic*. She specifically used the word *shame*.

During the difficult visit to the obstetrician, Beth had many questions, but couldn't stop crying long enough to ask them. Finally she confessed that she had always viewed pregnant single girls as either "incredibly stupid or incredibly selfish."

The obstetrician was quiet for a moment, then said, "...or they're incredibly human."

It was exactly the right thing to say—for Beth, for me, and now for you. Beth is carrying a child; you and I are carrying all sorts of things, too, but our baggage is usually less obvious. Some of what we carry is stupid and selfish, but what Beth carries is incredibly human. You would think we'd see the irony of that, but we do not. We march on doggedly, blind to our own faults and only too eager to shame others for their sins.

Maybe Beth should name her child after the obstetrician, but I already thought of other names. I think the baby should be called Wonderful. Or Counselor.

Sorry, I'm getting my Advent stories of pregnant single girls mixed up.

Then again, maybe not.

TRACK 12

That Thing with the Feathers

My old boss used to say to his employees, "We all get along like a family!" And I used to think to myself, "Man, do you know any families? Have you ever been in a family? Do you know what families are like?" Families are sometimes a mixed blessing, and my first-born and second-born daughters offer a prime example. The only other time I hear such caterwauling is on *Animal Planet*. Yes, Faith and Hope get along splendidly—until they don't, and then the chaos begins. After one particularly bruising encounter, I separated the combatants and suggested they tackle their homework instead of each other. I knew Faith had a speech due for her English class, and this is what she wrote—the most unexpected, most unmixed-blessing of all:

My sister Hope and I are close in age, but we're different in some ways—Hope likes different music than I do. She also dresses much "cooler" than I do. Plus, she can make me laugh more than anyone I know can. She can also make me feel better more than anyone else can. In some ways, Hope and I are opposites. While I can be uptight and critical, Hope can always be happy-go-lucky.

I'm making this tribute to Hope because I could not live without her. She is my other half, as clichéd as that sounds. I guess you could say, "There is no faith without hope," which applies not only to my sister and me but to life.

Emily Dickinson wrote:

'Hope' is the thing with feathers—
That perches in the soul—
And sings the tune without the words—
And never stops—at all—

I couldn't have said it better myself.

Neither could I. There's a certain natural tension in cramming five people into the same small house; leave it to Faith to remind me that "getting along like a family" is not meant to be perfectly harmonious or perfectly calm or perfect. It's meant to be that thing with the feathers that sings the tune without words, and never stops at all.

TRACK 13 > THE NAMES OF THOSE PLACES

TRACK 13A

Me Hitting Bottom

The following is a weak prayer, written during a weak moment by an even weaker pilgrim.

The morning began with my now-daily trip to the ICU, where my quadriplegic sister tries to fight off pneumonia with a ventilator and her own iron will. (If the image of a woman who can move only her elbows seems beyond tragic, add a respirator and take away her ability to speak. The human lexicon has no words for this. I've checked.)

Needless to say, I've had better mornings.

Which is worse—helplessness or rage? The former hurts, but the latter sticks. In my family's case, you'd think years of practice would give us an edge in this debate—we've had plenty of dress rehearsals for Cindy's death. If the average person spends two years of life waiting in lines, then my family has spent four decades waiting in drab-colored rooms with big windows and industrial carpet, waiting for visiting hours or blood tests or surgeons or answers or miracles. Mostly miracles.

And I've spent twice that time in church—an eternity, really—waiting and praying for miracles and answers. On days like today, sitting bumper-to-bumper on the Parkway East on my (late) way to work, prayer seems like an ill-timed joke, and God reminds me of a careless absentee landlord who's put me up in a windowless, cold-water flat with no heat and no chance at subletting—except maybe to my sister, who'd welcome the change.

In the past eighteen months, I've attended six funerals and uncounted hours of therapy. A couple bat mitzvahs provided some balance, but mostly it's been the sixth, seventh and eighth stages of grief: shots of whiskey, proffered casseroles from the neighbors and the ever-present, ever-sincere, ever-superfluous, "if-there's-anything-I-can-do." And I've learned a lot about myself in therapy—mostly I've discovered how emotionally immature I am, and how little I can do about it. Imagine a sudden ability to read music, but no skill to play an instrument. I know every note, but remain tone deaf. I have the insight, but not the wisdom.

That bouncing sound you hear is me hitting bottom.

Somewhere near the Squirrel Hill exit, I remember a line from the Book of Common Prayer: "Lord, save us from the presumption of coming to this table for solace only, and not for strength; for pardon only, and not for renewal." And I'd add another line: for peace only, and not for courage; for freedom from suffering, and not for responsibility. Lord, save me from the presumption of knowing what's best; save me from the presumption of knowing what's worst. Save me from the presumption of knowing.

Truth is, our time in waiting rooms has been borrowed time. My sister has survived forty-two years as a quadriplegic—a Las Vegas bookie would scoff at those odds. A doctor gave my dad the sad lesson in 1967: "Quads don't live long. Your daughter will make it five, maybe ten years." (Nice bedside manner, doc. Which is worse—helplessness or rage?) Instead my sister finished high school, finished college, and made a life for herself. She's battled pneumonia and insurance companies and doubt—especially doubt, the worst contagion of all. My mother and father and aunt and my brother and a cadre of nurses and neighbors have made this possible—but mostly it was my sister's simple refusal to die. And now she gives lessons to doctors, who must re-think their weighty calculus. She gives lessons to all of us—and not in the subjunctive case, not with the conditional "if you consider that's she's quadriplegic…" No. Forget the label. Tenacity is better than helplessness or rage, and tenacity knows no label. Tenacity is a choice, not a diagnosis. Tenacity is strength and courage and renewal and responsibility, where you wake up every morning and pack your lunch (casserole leftovers) and steer your car through whatever the traffic brings, maybe you find the occasional shortcut because maybe you're wiser than you think, maybe you realize that you don't need to know the word for everything, and maybe, with some guidance and some impromptu prayer, you can make it through another day.

The Worst Apostle Says Thank You

I am the worst apostle.

I'm a casual collector of miracles; by last count, I've garnered…I dunno…several, or several million, depending on accounting schemes. Traditionally I've been conservative, rendering only a few unqualified verdicts of astonishment. But something about that approach has made me both wary and jaded; now most everything has rote methodology, a checklist like fourth-grade science—"Add some baking powder to the beaker. What do you see? Write down your observations…and always wear your safety glasses."

My sister Cindy came home from the hospital yesterday. It was the usual transportation issue: medicine meets the grocery checkout line ("Does she have this? Do you need this? Don't forget the suction kit. Did we pay for that?") It's mechanical more than joyous. I'm happy she's home, I guess, aside from the endless worry.

And that's why I'm such a horrid apostle. I come bearing good news, but it's tainted. We survived the latest assault, but tomorrow might bring more disaster, and if not tomorrow then the next day. Eventually, of course, I'll be right, but what kind of a sucker's bet is that? Who wants to count meds instead of miracles? At what point do we take off the safety goggles and see life as it really is, clear-eyed despite the risks?

I don't know. I do know this: A month ago I dodged a nurse wheeling a crash cart into my sister's room. Three weeks ago the doctor told me it was "highly unlikely" Cindy would ever come off the ventilator, and perhaps it was time to make "long-term plans"— something other than her own home.

Yet come home she did. Eventually we all come home. Maybe the rooms are more crowded now (no ventilator, thank you), and there's the constant sound of whirring machines, the snoring sound of the next catastrophe, asleep in some unknown crevice in the corner of the room. Someday it'll awaken without prompting. But for now my sister is home where she belongs. The windows of her bedroom face west, and (I cannot make this up) you can see better sunsets from up there. Of course you have to look past the suction machine on the corner of her dresser, but I swear there is always an incredible sunset burning into the dusk out there. I can see it without my glasses: endless, joyous, improbable. A miracle, really.

The Names of Those Places

It has always troubled me that out of the five members of my birth family, I was the sixth-best writer. Everyone, including the dog, told better stories. My sister Cindy could tell stories—or at least finish them. When she found out that a well-known philanderer had lost his legs to diabetes, Cindy said, "Well, he won't be running around on his wife anymore..."

It's no small thing to tell good stories. It's how we make sense of the world. Stories serve as reality's butcher, slicing the fat and leaving the meat. Few good stories begin, *Well I woke up and had some oatmeal.* Good stories begin with *Well I woke up and had some bourbon* or *I told him that would be stupid but he didn't listen* or *Everything seemed OK until...*

The other thing that troubles me—that troubles any serious writer—is clichés. Clichés make for bad stories. Unlike bourbon, clichés lead to predictable endings with trite morals. We all nod approvingly, like we're saluting Mom or apple pie (but if the pie explodes in Mom's face—now *that's* a story).

The birth of Jesus is a great story—babe in swaddling clothes, star of wonder, shepherds, magi. Who *doesn't* like an infant cute as Christmas? But the death of Jesus—arms splayed and nailed, legs oddly bent, bloodless and vulnerable, asking for a drink of water and getting gall instead. Ah, yes. Well. Hmmm. Not pretty. No one wants that story.

My sister died recently. She was a quadriplegic. Her story has all the elements of a cliché: a treacly tear-jerker about a young woman who overcomes adversity and...cue the weepy music. Fill in your favorite moral here. It's true, but it's cheap. Clichés are all heart but no muscle. Forget who she was as a person—focus on the wheelchair, dammit!

Let me tell you a story. For the past forty-five years, my sister would wake up, but not to oatmeal or bourbon. She would wake to the knowledge that her paralysis—the result of a sledding accident at age twelve—had not left her overnight, that the pleasant dreams where she walked or ran or climbed trees would become nightmares upon waking, that she would once again face another day with a full and active mind but with legs oddly bent, splayed arms, relying on others for even the simplest of actions—for a drink of water, for a crust of bread, for compassion. Every minute Cindy spent reading or watching TV or taking classes at Pitt or writing emails (using a pencil between her teeth) took nine minutes of prep. And, to paraphrase Jackson Browne, when the morning light came streaming in, she'd get up and do it again. Amen. And her first question, her very first question every time she'd see us? "How are *you*? How are *you* doing?"

What is profound here is the lack of story. Look around you: By what measure would one judge this woman a success? Her money? Job? Standing? We can all say *Oh no, those things aren't important, no, no, it's her character.* Sure. Tell your spouse and your boss tomorrow that you're quitting your job to go build character. Everyone will admire you except the mortgage company. On second thought, no one will admire you.

What we lack isn't a story; what we lack is language. What's the name of the gap near the end of Beethoven's Ninth Symphony, that final pause before all hell breaks loose, before *Alle Menschen werden Brüder*? What's the name for the empty place in your heart where you whisper your most urgent prayers? What's the name for the spaces between *I* and *love* and *you*? What's the name for that sudden intake of breath when you hear those words, *Yes, I will marry you* or *We're expecting a baby* or *Your sister has died*? What are the names of those places?

I now know what fills those spaces, the names of those places. My mom owned a big part of those gaps; my dad, too—their corporate, unwavering dedication to their eldest child knew no bounds. My aunt was an enormous help. My wife and kids, who could have quite rightly felt resentful at my growing absences with each hospital visit, but instead showed nothing but love and compassion. My endlessly patient brother Kevin and his family. And there were relatives. Sandee's relatives. Nina. Mimi Blake. Mrs. Pasquarelli. The Carmelites. Amazing neighbors like the Milkos. And Helen and Arica, who were—let's face it—really sisters to Cindy, not just nurses. A thousand others—a litany of saints, known and unknown. Without them, the story of my sister is chaotic and senseless, a run-on sentence; with them, it's narrative. Flesh and blood. Meaning.

And some of those spaces have your name on them. You completed the web. You're thinking, *But I did nothing to help…*yet here you are at the end the story, the most important part where you learn what it all means, and there's your name, front and center: Every time (*every time*) you asked about my sister, you became a compassionate character in our collective story, filling those nameless spaces. Here you thought it was a story about Cindy but it's really a story about you: *How are you? How are you doing?*

Each morning my sister made a choice, the most clichéd and unclichéd choice. A random fracture of the C3/C4 vertebrae all those years ago left her with seemingly few choices, save the most vital, the most crucial one of all: We can live this life as it comes, meeting others *where* they are and *who* they are and not what they can do or what they look like or what they could be if only.

We can meet tragedy on its own court: We can choose to play—outmatched, outmuscled, except where it counts most—or we can take our ball and go home, safe in our own suffering. Cindy chose the former, difficult, tenacious path: to get up and do it again. I'd love to tell you she did so without complaint, but she was human. But she did so with a remarkable courage that was also human, which means it's available to us as well. It's our choice. We can choose to live on cheap morals of store-bought clichés, or we can write our names in those empty spaces in the lives of those around us. There are no guarantees we will win. None. But we will not lose.

We can choose to sit anchored in the harbor and harbor our grudges against life's outrageous misfortune. Or we can roll back the stone like Jesus did, unfurl the mast, untie the ropes. The plain fact is that our lives are pulling out of the dock right now, bound for open, nameless places, ready for us to scrawl our transient initials on fickle winds.

You want your name set in rock? Fine—go buy a tombstone. Otherwise hop aboard. Amen.

TRACK 14

Not Always

Outside my father-in-law's room, I heard a hospice nurse say, "We usually die the way we lived."

I have held on to what she said, specifically the word *usually*. Usually, as in *not always*. That means there's still a chance I *won't* die the way I lived: parked in traffic, standing in line, looking for my daughter's soccer shoes. ("No, Daddy, the *red* ones.") I won't die working on my car or filling out forms or watching stupid reruns. I won't die simply waiting waiting waiting...

Once, on a beach in Avalon, New Jersey, my father-in-law told me this joke: "I want to die like my great-great grandpa: peacefully, in his sleep...not like the screaming passengers in his wagon when he drove it into the river."

I laughed when he told me that, and that's how I want to go: eyes closed, head back, the sun on my face, throat full of happiness at the sheer absurd joy of it all, and hoping St. Peter's sense of humor is way more merciful than just.

TRACK 15

A River of Sin Called Denial

At any church service, Catholic or otherwise, I recite these eight words: *Lord, I am not worthy to receive you.* It was a humility instilled by my upbringing; more importantly, it has been reinforced by everyday experience from every day I have spent on this planet.

I am a sinner. The realization that I join the human race in that distinction provides no comfort. My sins have been personal, active, sober choices. (Okay, not *always* sober.) To blame them on everyone else is yet another sin.

I am also an environmentalist—a mighty hypocritical one, but still. To examine the global ecology with an open mind is to realize the breadth of our collective sin. Someone far brighter than me explained it this way:

> *Here is the truth about the Original Sin: humankind is relentlessly destructive. The human imagination is so diseased by sin that we defeat our own interests time and time again. We have depleted the fisheries from which we eat, poisoned the rivers from which we drink, and fouled even the air we breathe. Worst of all, we live denying these facts, which gives the full measure of our sinfulness.*

Yep, worst of all is denial. In the hierarchy of sin, the basest level is denying God's merciful bounty to our fellow astronauts on spaceship Earth. To squander the future for the present denies hope for God's children in coming generations. Trust me: There is a special circle in Hell (or at least a very long line in Purgatory) for souls with such hubris. Catholic or not, Christian or not, believer or not, we can't steal from the future and not pay the price. Nature always wins.

I bring up this public confession for a reason. The quotation above is from a work published by the U.S. Conference of Catholic Bishops. The Church in general and U.S. bishops in particular have had a bad run of late (some of it mightily deserved). It's important to put their work in context. U.S. prelates have long been at the forefront of radical political thought: War and suffering are bad, peace and justice good. In present politics, such ideas pass for "radical." What's more alarming: Jesus said things like this *all the time*. Pope Francis, in his encyclical, *Laudato Si*, doubled down on the bishops' statement: "The violence present in our hearts, wounded by sin, is also reflected in the symptoms of sickness evident in the soil, in the water, in the air and in all forms of life."

And so as a *practicing* (pun intended) Catholic I face a dilemma, and not the paper-vs-plastic kind. I am "wounded by sin," and must make choices that reflect the better angels of my nature so that I don't offend nature itself and commit the transgression that is, in the words of my bishops, "worst of all."

Such a choice, as John Henry Cardinal Newman said, is one of conscience. God created me with free will—a mixed blessing, but a blessing nonetheless. I can choose to help change the course of our society (where Americans make up five percent of the world's population and use twenty-five percent of its natural resources), or I can live as I have been living—in denial, as a plunderer, a sinner, a thief who nakedly steals from those next in line.

A final note. I don't just say *those* eight words—*Lord, I am not worthy to receive you*—every Sunday; I answer them with eleven more: *...but only say the word and my soul shall be healed.*

I have bet my salvation on those words, and I must answer to my God-given conscience every day for what I do to God's green earth.

TRACK 16

4:53 a.m.

At some point, at many points, you will be asked to start again. Check that: you won't be asked—you will be informed that your old life is over. A knock on the door. A telegram. The doctor will see you now. A baby will arrive, wet and crying. Or your daughter will wed, and *you'll* be crying. It'll happen. And, for the millionth time, you'll muster your resources—and for the millionth time they'll assemble family, friends, prayers, people…

…until one day when they won't. For some sudden reason, typically around 2:13 a.m., you're alone. Who knows why ? Bad timing, bad karma—but the folks you counted on aren't there. No malice aforethought; they just couldn't make it. And your prayers have come up empty, too—you feel like you're praying into the ether. No malice aforethought; it simply seems God couldn't make it either.

You feel you're all alone, but you're not utterly alone. Every prophet, every pauper has taken this journey—forty days adrift or forty days in the desert or forty years or 4,000. Cold comfort, really—misery loathes company. What did the Buddha conclude after years of enlightened contemplation? Life is suffering. Lovely.

But that's not the end of it. All of these lonely, painful journeys share something else: shedding your old self. Not only shedding the usual suspects (possessions, prepossessions, presumptions), but shedding your old way of thinking. Maybe your friends didn't abandon you; maybe they're on their own journey and you were too tired to lift your head from your own footfall to notice. Maybe having a child or losing a job makes you think you cannot—can not—soldier on…yet here you are reading this, soldiering on, against all odds.

And maybe that's where you find the divine—in the desert, in this new life that has emerged unasked, against all odds. And maybe that's grace: showing up unsolicited at 4:53 a.m., carrying solace as tenderly as one carries an infant. You see it now, in the rear-view mirror, as you trace your wayward tracks through the desert dust—and now that the dust has settled in front of you, you have some idea of where you're going. Against all odds.

Here is my prayer for you, the same prayer I whisper into the ether for myself: Pray to the God who's there. Pray to the God who you wish were there. Pray to the divine emptiness you feel—a bag of carbon and water hurtling through space, third rock from the sun. Pray for that dust-free, clear-eyed existential vision—and pray for change, the last horse of your apocalypse. You bet on that horse to show, but that horse always, always wins. That horse, that final horse will give you the final revelation: we're all alone…yet somehow, miraculously it's *we*, the we who house grace and holiness and divinity and redemption. Ironic, huh? Buffeted by change, the desert's rock tumbler has smoothed our jagged edges into outrageous, unique, ridiculous bits of beauty that we are, that you are. No guru, no method, no teacher, said Van Morrison—just us: shell-shocked but together, a little wiser, flecks of heavenly carbon shining in the sun, against all odds, alive, alone-but-not-alone, amen.

It's everything you asked for.

It's everything you didn't ask for.

It's everything. Shalom.

BONUS TRACK

The Pope's Mechanic

[Pope Francis] took possession of a nearly 30-year-old Renault 4L which… was given to the pope by the Rev. Renzo Zocca, a 69-year-old Italian parish priest.

Good Morning America

TO: His Holiness Pope Francis <francisthe1@vatican.it.>
FROM: Luigi@Luigisgarage.it
RE: His Holiness' Renault 4L

Your Most Blessed Holiness,

Greetings from your most humble servant. I am so thrilled that you chose my modest garage for your car needs. I was…surprised by your choice of car (a 29-year-old Renault for *il Pape*?), and even more surprised that you chose Luigi's Garage for your service needs. Thank you for this honor. It has 186,000 miles on it! Another minor miracle for Your Holiness!

As you noted, there seems to be a small over-heating problem. Although white smoke is good in your line of work, it's not so good for a Renault. Of course we will solve this issue and I'll return the car promptly. No charge for you, of course.

TO: francisthe1@vatican.it.
FROM: Luigi@Luigisgarage.it

Your Holiness,

I'm always happy to drop whatever I'm doing for one of your many visits. As you said, the smoke problem went away but was replaced by a brake problem. I understand you wear the "The Shoes of the Fisherman"—apparently Renault used those same first-century leather shoes on all four brakes. No charge this time.

TO: His Holiness Pope Francis <francisthe1@vatican.it.>
FROM: Luigi@Luigisgarage.it

Holiness,

I understand you got this car from a friend of yours—he must've followed your adage, "It's better to give than to receive." I've done some research, and Renault called the 4L's cooling system "mechanically simple and very effective." So was the guillotine, but we don't use that anymore either. I am fashioning something more workable. I guess my other (paying) customers will have to wait—which, of course, they would be honored to do for a customer like you.

TO: His Holiness Pope Francis <francisthe1@vatican.it.>
FROM: Luigi@Luigisgarage.it

YH,

I figured out why the electrical system went to ~~hell~~ heck: A family of feral vermin were living (and eating) in your ductwork. Quite the feisty family—they took turns biting me as I attempted their removal. I was going to dispatch them, but my wife reminded me that you took your name after Francis of Assisi, a friend to animals. The cute little buggers are now living in my garage. The car awaits your pick up. I can't afford to lose any more time driving to your place. Besides, the Swiss guards have started making fun of me.

TO: His Holiness Pope Francis <francisthe1@vatican.it.>
FROM: Luigi@Luigisgarage.it

Padre,

Mea culpa—I bled on your front bumper. The hood latch is conveniently located at forehead height; I opened a nice gash across my now-receding hairline.

I beginning to think this vehicle may be the ultimate revenge of *les papes d'Avignon*. It makes people in other countries surrender first for a change. Please find my invoice enclosed.

TO: His Holiness Pope Francis <francisthe1@vatican.it.>
FROM: Luigi@Luigisgarage.it

Francis,

Please excuse last night's email asking if you perform vehicular exorcisms. I was tired, but I truly believe the "L" in 4L stands for Lucifer. I am at my wit's end. Last night I dreamt I was being chased by the Renault through St. Peter's Square—the 4L's head gasket spun around, spewing green antifreeze.

TO: His Holiness Pope Francis <francisthe1@vatican.it.>
FROM: Luigi@Luigisgarage.it

Frank,

This piece of junk will be the end of me. My hands are so bloodied I look like I have the stigmata. I've used the Lord's name in vain so many times I now speak in tongues. Dante's hell had ten circles; mine goes to eleven.

P.S. I guillotined all of the vermin just to watch them die.

TO: His Holiness Pope Francis <francisthe1@vatican.it.>
FROM: Luigi@Luigisgarage.it

Frankie!

Greetings from Santa Lucia! The psychiatric wing here has a wonderful view of the Aegean Sea. Sometimes, when my medication is just right, they'll let me visit the veranda—but not in a wheelchair. I'm apparently not quite ready for anything with wheels.

I suppose I should tell you I'm sorry I drove the 4L into the canal. Actually, I'm not sorry, but I can't get out of here until I apologize. So let me apologize for taking so long to drive your car into a canal.

Have to go. Time for Arts and Crafts. I'm halfway through building a scale model of the Renault so I can set it on fire and throw it into the Aegean.

Your former mechanic,
Luigi

NOTES

All biblical quotations from *The Holy Bible, King James Version.*
Cambridge Edition: 1769; *King James Bible Online*, 2016.

Annie Dillard quotation appears in the essay "Total Eclipse," from
Teaching a Stone to Talk, Harper & Row, 1982.

Emily Dickinson poem on page 81 is from *The Poems of Emily
Dickinson*, edited by Thomas H. Johnson, Cambridge, Mass.: The
Belknap Press of Harvard University Press, Copyright © 1951,
1955, 1979, 1983 by the President and Fellows of Harvard College.

Quote from "An Ecological Spirituality" by Rev. Joseph A.
Tetlow, SJ / U.S. Conference of Catholic Bishops,
http://wwwmigrate.usccb.org/issues-and-action/human-life-and-
dignity/environment/an-ecological-spirituality.cfm

ACKNOWLEDGMENTS
AND DEDICATION

The following is a weak prayer...written by an even weaker pilgrim:

To friends and family not named here: I am outnumbered and humbled by your solace, trust and support.

To Brian Doyle, Mike Kane, and Michael Coyne for their invaluable advice on getting this published; to Steph Samoy for her amazing and generous encouragement; to readers and editors of *Daily Guideposts, Pitt Magazine,* and the Pittsburgh *Post-Gazette* for their kind words.

To Jessica Titler, who edited the introduction as part of a class project on editing at the University of Pittsburgh [Ellen Smith, instructor].

To my in-laws and outlaws: thank you, most of the time.

To my colleagues at the University of Pittsburgh: I appreciate your patience. To my students, past and present: You deserve a better teacher, and you have made me a better person. (Speaking of patience: Thank you, Robin.)

To the folks on the dek-hockey team: You really deserve someone better than me...someone with, I dunno, skill. Or knees, maybe.

To my sister, aunt, and mom for everything.

To my father, who died while this book was being born—thank you.

To my brother: It's me and you, bud.

To Faith, Hope, and Grace, my manna from heaven: For my next writing project, I'll work on a new vocabulary—inventing words that might begin to approximate what you have meant to me.

And to Sandee, indubitably the most complex, fascinating, exasperating, gifted person I have ever met, my life-long, puzzling, and holy companion...this is for you.

Other Books from In Extenso Press

ALL THINGS TO ALL PEOPLE: A Catholic Church for the
Twenty-First Century, by Louis DeThomasis, FSC, 118 pages, paperback

CATHOLIC BOY BLUES: A Poet's Journey of Healing,
by Norbert Krapf, 224 pages, paperback

CATHOLIC WATERSHED: The Chicago Ordination Class of 1969
and How They Helped Change the Church, by Michael P. Cahill,
394 pages, paperback

CHRISTIAN CONTEMPLATIVE LIVING
Six Connecting Points, by Thomas M. Santa CSSR, 126 pages, paperback

GREAT MEN OF THE BIBLE: A Guide for Guys
by Martin Pable, OFM Cap, 216 pages, paperback

THE GROUND OF LOVE AND TRUTH: Reflections on
Thomas Merton's Relationship with the Woman Known as "M,"
by Suzanne Zuercher, OSB, 120 pages, paperback

HOPE: One Man's Journey of Discovery from Tormented Child to Social
Worker to Spiritual Director, by Marshall Jung, 172 pages, paperback

MASTER OF CEREMONIES: A Novel
by Donald Cozzens, 288 pages, paperback and hardcover

NAVIGATING ALZHEIMER'S: 12 Truths about Caring for Your
Loved One, by Mary K. Doyle, 112 pages, paperback

THE SILENT SCHISM: Healing the Serious Split in the Catholic
Church by Louis DeThomasis, FSC, and Cynthia A. Nienhaus, CSA,
128 pages, paperback

THE UNPUBLISHED POET: On Not Giving Up on Your Dream
by Marjorie L. Skelly, 160 pages, paperback

WE THE (LITTLE) PEOPLE, artwork by ISz, 50 plates, paperback

YOUR SECOND TO LAST CHAPTER: Creating a Meaningful Life on
Your Own Terms, by Paul Wilkes, 120 pages, paperback and hardcover

AVAILABLE FROM BOOKSELLERS
OR FROM 800-397-2282
INEXTENSOPRESS.COM

DISTRIBUTED EXCLUSIVELY BY ACTA PUBLICATIONS